"The Gospels are biographies of how Jesus walked. Why do we read biographies? To learn how to live. Who better to learn from than Jesus? Jordan Raynor's paradigm of purpose, presence, and productivity is excellent. But learning it from Jesus? That's the magic."

—John Mark Comer, bestselling author
of *The Ruthless Elimination of Hurry*

"Mixing the theological and the tactical, Jordan Raynor offers a deeply original and practical take on time management, busyness, and the human urge toward living meaningfully."

—Cal Newport, *New York Times* bestselling author
of *A World Without Email* and *Deep Work*

"If wisdom had weight, this book would weigh a thousand pounds. Jordan Raynor gets it because he does it, and then he shows us all how to do it too. This book is honest, practical, and deeply actionable."

—Jon Acuff, *New York Times* bestselling author
of *Soundtracks: The Surprising Solution to Overthinking*

"What can we learn about time management from the life of Christ? It turns out, quite a lot! I'm so grateful Jordan has written this book."

—Janeen Uzzell, COO of Wikipedia

"For far too many of us, life feels like the meaningless passage of time between far too few meaningful moments. In this book, Jordan is your guide to a better way, giving you a highly practical road map to 'redeeming the time, because the days are evil' (Ephesians 5:16, NKJV)."

—Mark Batterson, *New York Times* bestselling author
of *The Circle Maker* and lead pastor of National Community Church

"In *Redeeming Your Time*, Jordan Raynor provides an outstanding guidebook to help you steward your time in ways that will make you more effective, productive, and content. Time is a gift from God, and we are called to be faithful stewards of it. *Redeeming Your Time* offers inspiration, tools, and tips to help you steward and maximize your gift of time. Jordan's insights will transform the way you view time and help you focus on the highest priorities in your life."

—Dee Ann Turner, bestselling author of *Bet on Talent* and *Crush Your Career*, and former vice president of talent and sustainability at Chick-fil-A

"Balance is not something you just achieve. It must be designed. In *Redeeming Your Time*, Jordan shows you how to design a simplified schedule that works for you!"

—Emily Ley, bestselling author of *A Simplified Life*

"Jordan Raynor is the master chief of productivity. In *Redeeming Your Time*, he has upped the ante on what it means to be truly productive as Christians. This book will not only change how you work but will also change how you view productivity as a whole."

—John Brandon, *Forbes* columnist and author
of *The 7-Minute Productivity Solution*

"Part of our response to the gospel is to manage our time wisely so we can serve others with excellence. This book will show you how."

—Horst Schulze, cofounder of the Ritz-Carlton
and author of *Excellence Wins*

"This book is a unique blend of theology, science, and practical tactics to help you redeem your time!"

—Dr. Caroline Leaf, *New York Times* bestselling author of
Switch On Your Brain

"I have read countless books on time management, yet none have left me transformed the way Jordan's God-given insight in *Redeeming Your Time* has. Within just five minutes of reading it, I found myself with both paradigm-shifting concepts and practical takeaways that I could instantly begin applying to my life. Highly recommend."

—Bob Lotich, author of *Simple Money, Rich Life*
and host of the *SeedTime Money* podcast

"Jordan Raynor has accomplished the rare feat of writing a thoughtful, theological, and highly practical book on how to manage your time. Best yet, he's got a track record that demonstrates his approach works. If you want to get better at leading yourself, you'll love *Redeeming Your Time*."

—Carey Nieuwhof, author of *At Your Best*, podcast host, and speaker

"Jordan Raynor is one of my favorite authors. His writing is always jam-packed with unique insights and deeply practical wisdom while always being rigorously biblical. This book is the only productivity book you will ever need to read. I have read many and only wish that Jordan had written this book sooner. *Redeeming Your Time* will give you a vision for a wildly productive life that fulfills God's purposes while avoiding the usual pitfalls. If you want to flourish, you don't want to miss this book!"

—Daniel Fusco, pastor of Crossroads Community Church, author
of *Crazy Happy*, and host of the TV show *Real with Daniel Fusco*

"We can make more money and we can buy more stuff, but we can't make or buy more time. In an era where people are wasting more and more time on things that have less and less importance, Jordan

Raynor's book is calling us back to focus on what really matters and equipping us to make every moment count."

—Nona Jones, bestselling author of *Success from the Inside Out* and head of faith-based partnerships for Facebook

"In *Redeeming Your Time*, Jordan has connected the best ideas on time management into one cohesive, gospel-centered approach. This is a large step forward for the entire field of time management. I am so grateful for this book!"

—Matt Perman, bestselling author of *What's Best Next: How the Gospel Transforms the Way You Get Things Done* and director of career development at the King's College

"Jordan has the amazing ability to combine deep and compelling theology with powerful data-driven insights. A one-two punch that makes this book powerful and hard to put down! Such a needed message!"

—Jefferson Bethke, *New York Times* bestselling author of *Take Back Your Family*

"Jordan does a masterful job of showing how the gospel is our source of ambition and rest. Looking for a Christlike approach to productivity? Look no further than *Redeeming Your Time*."

—Brad Lomenick, author of *H3 Leadership*

"An operating system from the life of Jesus—that's what Jordan's book is about. No wonder it leads to purpose, presence, and more productivity."

—Jeff Henderson, author of *Know What You're FOR* and founding lead pastor of Gwinnett Church

"*Redeeming Your Time* is full of biblical wisdom and common sense. It is the book I wish someone had given me when I started my business career."

—Hugh Whelchel, executive director of the Institute for Faith, Work & Economics and author of *How Then Should We Work?*

"*Redeeming Your Time* is equal parts theologically rich and practically attainable. When we recognize that Christ is not only our example for successful time management but also our reason for it, everything in life starts finding its proper place. Distractions stop owning our days, which allows us to grow in devotion to the One who does."

—Wendy Speake, author of *The 40-Day Social Media Fast*

"I've often prayed that God would give me direction on how to manage my time better. I never had enough paper for my to-do list. I tried waking up earlier, going to bed later, saying no, selling things, but none of that gave me the freedom I was looking for. After reading *Redeeming Your Time,* I learned that the perfecter of time management is Jesus Christ. He modeled what we can do in our everyday lives to glorify God while serving our spouses, kids, career, and communities. I am now equipped with biblical principles and proven strategies to help me redeem my time. I loved the book and I am sure you will too!"

—David Ragan, NASCAR driver

"The only truly limited resource for any leader is time. Jordan offers a gift to the leaders battling hustle, hurry, and haste with a gospel-centric master class in realizing true peace, purpose, and productivity. Thoughtful, practical, and powerfully anchored in the life and truth of Jesus—this book could alter the entire legacy of a leader."

—Mike Sharrow, CEO of C12

"The key to effectiveness is intentionality. In *Redeeming Your Time,* Jordan shows you how to model Jesus's intentionality so that you can be more purposeful, present, and productive. If you are looking for a way to excel in the thing God made you to do, this book will show you how!"

—Tamika Catchings, four-time Olympic gold medalist,
ten-time WNBA All-Star, and former WNBA MVP

"*Redeeming Your Time* lands like a life ring in the stormy seas of modern work. It helped me catch a breath when I needed one most. As someone with a very full schedule, a company to run, a family, and many personal commitments, I know the toll that is taken on professionals in the current ever-changing world of work. What astounds me, however, is that Jordan's schedule is much fuller than mine, yet he navigates the fullness and complexity of what he does with poise and focus that I only wish I had. In *Redeeming Your Time,* Jordan digs beyond surface-level time-management hacks that so many of us have tried and abandoned. His aim is not simply to help us find more time but to expose the root of our struggle and help us redeem one of the most precious things we have: the very minutes we have on earth."

—Sam Eitzen, cofounder of Snapbar

"If you don't have time to read a book on time, make time to read this one. Every chapter is a candid conversation with a gospel-centered mentor who is in the trenches with you. Jordan conversationally moves back and forth between theological wisdom and tactical tips, so you'll walk away with both the deep-rooted why and the daily how to make the most of the time God gives you."

—Michelle Myers, founder of she works His way

"Jordan Raynor teaches us to invest rather than spend time. As Einstein's relativistic physics taught us, time is elastic and bendy and pliable. In a poetic way, Jordan teaches us how to mold time to meet the things of eternity. Jordan was born for such a *time* as this."

—Ben Courson, founder of Hope Generation and bestselling author
of *Flirting with Darkness*

"We all want to be more purposeful, present, and productive, but sadly most of us don't really know where to start. *Redeeming Your Time* is the ultimate road map!"

—Patrice Washington, host of the *Redefining Wealth* podcast

"As Christ followers, we need to approach time management and productivity through a theological and worshipful lens. Jordan serves us well by leading the way."

—Ruth Chou Simons, *Wall Street Journal* bestselling author of *Beholding and Becoming* and *GraceLaced,* artist, and founder of gracelaced.com

"This book is a game changer. Plain and simple, if you take the principles within this book to heart and commit to practicing them, then you can expect your life (and the way you manage your time) to change in radical ways. Get ready to scribble down notes, highlight sections, and cling to the additional resources. This is a book to keep on the shelf and reread whenever you need to fine-tune the way you're spending your time."

—Hannah Brencher, author of *Fighting Forward* and *Come Matter Here*

"I read this book cover to cover in just one sitting . . . I couldn't put it down! In an age where most of us feel like we can barely slow down long enough to read anything over 140 characters, that should serve as a testament to just how good, wise, important, and timely this book really is. Jordan's words are the sharpening iron of a trusted friend, pointing us back to our true purpose with a gentle reminder of just how fleeting time really is. For all of us who long to make a kingdom-level impact with our gifts, our stories, our time—but find ourselves lost in an ever-increasingly noisy and distracted world—*Redeeming Your Time* is the handbook for taking back the 'good work' God has prepared for us in advance. This book is the wake-up call that a stretched-thin digital generation has been waiting for!"

—Mary Marantz, bestselling author of *Dirt* and host of *The Mary Marantz Show*

"Thank God this book exists! In *Redeeming Your Time,* Jordan has expertly balanced both the philosophical and the practical solutions for this chaotic and busy world we live in. As someone who struggles to find the line between rest and ambition, I was encouraged to see how Jesus models both and invites us to do the same. I highly recommend you take Jordan's advice and dissent from the kingdom of noise all around you—just make this book the exception!"

—Graham Cochrane, author of *How To Get Paid for What You Know*

"If you truly desire a life of purpose and meaning . . . take your *time* to learn this operating system that helps you live more like Jesus. *Redeeming Your Time* offers you a new sacred way to live in this frantic world of busyness."

—Michael Arrieta, CEO of Garden City Companies and former DocuSign executive

REDEEMING YOUR TIME

REDEEMING YOUR TIME

---

*7 Biblical Principles for Being Purposeful,
Present, and Wildly Productive*

JORDAN RAYNOR

WATERBROOK

Grateful acknowledgment is made to the following for permission to print excerpts from their interviews with the author:

Shay Cochrane: Interview with Jordan Raynor, September 24, 2020. Used by permission of Shay Cochrane.

Brett Hagler: Interview with Jordan Raynor in *The Call to Mastery* podcast, April 22, 2020. Used by permission of Brett Hagler.

Timothy J. Keller, Founding Pastor Emeritus, Redeemer Presbyterian Church of NYC: Interview with Jordan Raynor in *The Call to Mastery* podcast, April 15, 2020. Used by permission of Timothy J. Keller, Founding Pastor Emeritus, Redeemer Presbyterian Church of NYC.

Luke LeFevre: Interview with Jordan Raynor in *The Call to Mastery* podcast, January 29, 2020. Used by permission of Luke LeFevre.

Joel Manby: Interview with Jordan Raynor in *The Call to Mastery* podcast, May 6, 2020. Used by permission of Joel Manby.

Library of Congress Cataloging-in-Publication Data
Names: Raynor, Jordan, 1986– author.
Title: Redeeming your time : 7 biblical principles for being purposeful, present, and wildly productive / Jordan Raynor.
Description: First edition. | Colorado Springs : WaterBrook, [2021] | Includes bibliographical references.
Identifiers: LCCN 2021028046 | ISBN 9780593193075 (hardcover) | ISBN 9780593193082 (ebook)
Subjects: LCSH: Time management—Religious aspects—Christianity.
Classification: LCC BV4598.5 .R39 2021 | DDC 640/.43—dc23
LC record available at https://lccn.loc.gov/2021028046

Printed in the United States of America on acid-free paper

waterbrookmultnomah.com

4th Printing

First Edition

Interior book design by Fritz Metsch

SPECIAL SALES Most WaterBrook books are available at special quantity discounts when purchased in bulk by corporations, organizations, and special-interest groups. Custom imprinting or excerpting can also be done to fit special needs. For information, please email specialmarketscms@penguinrandomhouse.com.

*Dedicated to the giants whose shoulders
I stood on to write this book:*

*John Mark Comer, Cal Newport,
David Allen, Matt Perman, Kevin DeYoung,
Jen Wilkin, Emily P. Freeman, Tim Keller,
and N. T. Wright*

CONTENTS

INTRODUCTION: The Solution to Being Swamped xvii

CHAPTER 1: Start with the Word 1

Practice 1: Spend Time with the Author of Time

Practice 2: Pray What You Know

CHAPTER 2: Let Your Yes Be Yes 22

Practice 1: Choose a Workflow

Practice 2: Commit to a Single Commitment Tracking System

Practice 3: Collect Your Open Loops

Practice 4: Define Your Work

Practice 5: Maintain Your Commitment Tracking System

CHAPTER 3: Dissent from the Kingdom of Noise 52

Practice 1: Let Your Friends Curate Information for You

Practice 2: Stop Swimming in Infinity Pools

Practice 3: Choose More Filtered Content

Practice 4: Renounce or Attain Independence from Social Media

Practice 5: Parent Your Phone

Practice 6: Get Comfortable with the Crevices of Your Day

Practice 7: Take a Walk

Practice 8: Write to Think

Practice 9: Put the Quiet Back in Quiet Time

CHAPTER 4: Prioritize Your Yeses 78

> *Practice 1: Accept Your Mission*
>
> *Practice 2: Choose Your Callings*
>
> *Practice 3: Set Epic Long-Term Goals*
>
> *Practice 4: Draft Quarterly Goals*
>
> *Practice 5: Refine Your Projects Lists and Actions Lists*
>
> *Practice 6: Lock Posteriorities in the Basement*

CHAPTER 5: Accept Your "Unipresence" 100

> *Practice 1: Take Control of When You Check Messages*
>
> *Practice 2: Eliminate External Distractions*
>
> *Practice 3: Schedule Deep-Work Appointments with Yourself*
>
> *Practice 4: Create Space for the Shallows and Serendipity*

CHAPTER 6: Embrace Productive Rest. 129

> *Practice 1: Break Well Every Other Hour*
>
> *Practice 2: Create an Eight-Hour Sleep Opportunity Every Night*
>
> *Practice 3: Cease and Feast Once a Week*

CHAPTER 7: Eliminate All Hurry. 155

> *Practice 1: Build a Time Budget Template*
>
> *Practice 2: Adjust Your Time Budget in a Daily Review*
>
> *Practice 3: Protect Your Time Budget with a Unique Approach to "No"*

EPILOGUE: The Dark Side of Discipline 191

ACKNOWLEDGMENTS 195

NOTES 197

THE SOLUTION TO BEING SWAMPED

'm *swamped*."

I've said it, you've said it—we've all said it at one point or
another. Maybe you're in a season of feeling swamped right now.
You roll out of bed each morning exhausted from not getting enough
sleep. You pull open your phone to find a dozen text messages, from
the ridiculous (another GIF of a dancing dog) to the exhausting ("Can
you bring Chloe home from church tonight?"). If you manage to
squeeze in a few minutes of "quiet time," you're quickly interrupted
by your calendar notifying you of today's meeting that you didn't have
enough time to fully prepare for.

At work, the struggle continues. Your to-do list seems to be getting
longer, not shorter. Your day is filled with back-to-back meetings, with
no time to think in between. When you are finally able to carve out
some time to focus on some "real work," that familiar ambient anxiety
creeps in, leading you to question if the project you're working on is
the "right thing" for you to be focused on at that moment.

After work, you rush back home to have dinner with your family or
friends. Sitting across from the people you care about the most, you're
there but not really *there*, as your brain is trying to do the thinking
you didn't have time to do during the day. After dinner, it's the mad
rush of all rushes: clean up, help the kids with their homework, and
pray that everyone finds time for a bath. After streaming your favorite
show, studying for an exam, or cramming in a few minutes of reading,
you check email one last time and go to bed, only to wake up and do
it all over again the next day.

Sound familiar? Of course, this is an extreme picture of what it looks like to be swamped, but I'm afraid it's closer to reality than most of us care to admit. Increasingly, it feels like time happens *to* us—like we're running a race that's impossible to win. We feel beholden to our calendars, watches, and to-do lists rather than having dominion over these tools that promised to make our lives easier and more productive. We have too much to do and not nearly enough time to do it. In short, we're swamped.

The Bible tells us that more than two thousand years ago, Jesus's disciples were "swamped" in a different way. Luke 8:22–23 records the scene:

> One day Jesus said to his disciples, "Let us go over to the other side of the lake." So they got into a boat and set out. As they sailed, he fell asleep. A squall came down on the lake, so that the boat was being swamped, and they were in great danger.

The disciples were out there on the lake, enjoying a quiet sail with Jesus, when all of a sudden, things spiraled out of control. You can imagine the boat taking on water from every side while the disciples frantically try to bail the water out, only to look back and see *more* water than before. (Sounds a lot like our never-ending to-do lists, am I right?) Luke says, "The boat was being swamped," leaving the disciples with only one thing to do. Recognizing they couldn't calm the chaos on their own, the disciples woke Jesus up and begged him to help. Verse 24 shares what happened next: "[Jesus] got up and rebuked the wind and the raging waters; the storm subsided, and all was calm."

This passage perfectly illustrates the core premise of this book—namely, that the solution to the disciples' being swamped by the wind and waves is the exact same solution to our being swamped by our to-do lists and hurried schedules. The solution to our perennial struggle with time management is found in Jesus Christ. How? In two ways.

*The solution to our perennial struggle with time
management is found in Jesus Christ.*

First, *Jesus offers you peace before you do anything.* Nearly every time-management expert says that the path to peace and productivity is found in implementing his or her system. This is what we might call "works-based productivity," which claims that *if* you do exercises X, Y, and Z, *then* you will find peace. This book begins with the opposite premise, in what we might call "grace-based productivity," which says that through Jesus Christ, we *already have* peace, and we do time-management exercises X, Y, and Z as a response of worship.

Again, look at the disciples in the swamped boat. They didn't do anything to calm the chaos. They merely trusted Jesus to still the storm. You and I can do the same. By trusting in Jesus for the forgiveness of our sins, we have "peace with God" (Romans 5:1) that is secure regardless of how productive we are or how well we steward our time. Matt Perman, a former member of John Piper's staff and the bestselling author of *What's Best Next,* wrote that for Christians "peace comes first, not second. The mistake we often make is to make peace of mind the result of things we do rather than the source."[1]

Don't get me wrong—in this book, you're going to learn how to do *a lot* of practical things that transform you from feeling swamped to feeling peaceful and productive. But the tactics in this book will *never* be your most foundational source of peace. If they were, this book would be guaranteed to fail you at some point. As Christians, our ultimate source of peace—our ultimate solution to being swamped—is found in the God-man sleeping through the storm. As the apostle Paul said in Ephesians 2:14, "[Jesus] himself is our peace."

Here's the second way that Jesus is the solution to our time-management problems: *he shows us how God would manage his time.* This is a *wild* idea if you think about it, and we're going to unpack it at length in chapter 1. No, the gospel biographies do not show Jesus walking around with a to-do list, calendar, or smartwatch. But as we'll see throughout this book, the Gospels *do* show him prioritizing where he spent his time (see Mark 1:38), dealing with distractions at work (see Matthew 12:46–50), fighting for silence (see 14:13), and seeking to be busy without being hurried (see Mark 11:11). In other words, the Gospels show Jesus facing many of the same challenges we face today as we seek to steward our time. And because he was infallible God, we can assume that Jesus managed his time *perfectly,* providing us with the ideal model to follow.

DOES THE WORLD REALLY NEED ANOTHER TIME-MANAGEMENT BOOK?

I've read more than forty books on time management and productivity, including all the enduring bestsellers in this category. But that doesn't even scratch the surface of the *thousands* of books that have been published on this topic. If the time-management category is already so cluttered, why write this book? What makes *this* book different? I have three answers to that question.

First, *this book accounts for how the Author of time managed his time.* Jesus was the most productive person who ever lived, yet nearly every time-management book fails to address how he spent his time on earth. That's crazy! We'd be foolish not to study his lifestyle and the habits that led to his being so purposeful, present, and productive. I know you might not think the Gospels have much to say about how Jesus managed his time, but I promise they do. More on this in chapter 1.

Second, unlike most time-management titles, *this book seeks to collect and connect the previously disconnected pieces of the time-management puzzle.* Prior to writing this book, when people would ask me for advice on how to best manage their time, I would recommend *nearly a dozen* different books for them to read.* Of course, that's the *last* thing a swamped person wants to hear. When you're overwhelmed, you barely have enough time to read *one* book, much less twelve! So why would I recommend so many books? Because each of those excellent titles deals with a critical piece of the time-management puzzle, but no single book contains all the pieces and links them together. My audacious goal is to zero in on the practices from these books that have worked for me and connect them together into a cohesive whole.

Finally, *this book attempts to create a unique balance between the theological, the theoretical, and the tactical.* In my experience, most time-management books overcompensate toward one of these three extremes. They're either so pie-in-the-sky that you can't *do* anything with them, or they're so dry that it feels like you're drinking sand.† In this book, I seek to strike a happy medium. But before I tell you *how* I plan to do this, I want to address an important question.

WHY SHOULD YOU TRUST ME WITH YOUR TIME?

There's no such thing as a PhD in time management, so how can you decide which alleged guru to trust? You have to rely on the *perspective* and *productivity* of your potential guide.

---

*If you're curious, I have included that list of books here. Each of these books is outstanding. I would encourage you to read each, as time permits: *Getting Things Done* by David Allen, *Deep Work* by Cal Newport, *The Way We're Working Isn't Working* by Tony Schwartz, *The Sabbath* by Abraham Joshua Heschel, *Essentialism* by Greg McKeown, *Digital Minimalism* by Cal Newport, *What's Best Next* by Matt Perman, *Measure What Matters* by John Doerr, *The 4-Hour Workweek* by Tim Ferriss, *Why We Sleep* by Matthew Walker, and *The Ruthless Elimination of Hurry* by John Mark Comer.

†Yes, that's an homage to one of Aaron Sorkin's greatest rants in *The American President,* the precursor to my all-time favorite, *The West Wing.*

My perspective on time management is shaped by the gospel of Jesus Christ. There's a big difference between a book that is biblically based and one that is gospel centric. My aim is the latter. As you'll see in chapter 1, the gospel is our ultimate source of ambition *and* rest, and that truth has tremendous practical applications for how we redeem our time.

But my perspective isn't enough reason for you to trust me. If I were you, I'd also want to know how productive I am as I practice what I'm going to preach throughout this book. Here's a summary of some of the things God has done through me over the past five years: As an entrepreneur, I've built two sizable businesses and created more than a hundred jobs. As a writer, I've signed seven book deals and helped more than three million Christians in every country connect the gospel with their work. At home, I've lost fifty pounds (and kept it off), been raising my daughters (currently ages six, four, and one), baptized my eldest, and grown a thriving marriage with my bride. In short, I think I've had a productive five-year run.

But let me make one thing crystal clear: *I am not the hero in this story.* God is. Deuteronomy 8:18 reminds us that it is "[God] who gives [us] the ability to produce wealth" and results. Over the years, God has graciously given me a wealth of knowledge and experience in stewarding my time well. Now I want to help you do the same. I want to help you redeem your time.

WHAT DOES IT MEAN TO REDEEM YOUR TIME?

The gospel is at the heart of this book, and it's also at the heart of the book of Ephesians, where the concept of redeeming our time comes from. After expounding upon the gospel of grace in Ephesians 1–4, the apostle Paul reminded us of our status as "dearly loved children" of God in Ephesians 5:1. What is our response to our adoption as sons and daughters of God? Paul answered that question a few verses later, saying,

See then that you walk circumspectly, not as fools but as wise, redeeming the time, because the days are evil.

Therefore do not be unwise, but understand what the will of the Lord is. (verses 15–17, NKJV)

Paul was saying that part of our response to the gospel is to redeem our time—to manage our time as carefully and wisely as possible. The Greek word *exagorazó,* which we translate to mean "redeeming" in "redeeming the time," literally means to "buy up" or "ransom."[2] If you've ever said, "I wish I could buy more time," *that's* the idea here. As Christians, we are called to "buy up" as much time as we can. Commenting on this passage, Timothy Keller said, "Christians are solemnly obliged not to waste time. Time-stewardship is a command!"[3]

Part of our response to the gospel is to redeem our time— to manage our time as carefully and wisely as possible.

Why are we commanded to redeem our time? Not so we will have more time to spend on selfish pursuits. We are called to redeem our time because "the days are evil" and we are running out of time to do "the will of the Lord." One of my favorite Bible teachers, Jen Wilkin, put it this way: "We are commanded to be time redeemers, those who reclaim our time from useless pursuits and employ it to the glory of God."[4] Amen. We don't redeem our time so we can "be more successful." If that's the book you're looking for, you can put this one down right now. Success isn't our primary aim—*service* is, and more specifically service to our Lord and his agenda.

Success isn't our primary aim—service is, and more specifically service to our Lord and his agenda.

So, what is his agenda? Why should you care about redeeming your time? Because redeeming your time allows you to do more "good works" for others that bring glory to God (see Matthew 5:16, ESV), create for his eternal kingdom (see 1 Corinthians 15:58), "make disciples" (Matthew 28:19), impress the Lord's commands on your children (see Deuteronomy 6:6–7), and enjoy God and his good blessings (see Philippians 4:4).

Okay, so we're called to redeem our time to do "the will of the Lord." But *how* do we do that? That's what this book is all about.

A GUIDE TO THIS BOOK

Each of the seven chapters in this book is broken into two distinct parts: principles and practices.

Principles

The subtitle of this book promises seven biblical principles for being purposeful, present, and wildly productive. The first part of each chapter will introduce you to one of these seven principles, each drawn from the life or commands of Jesus Christ. Prior to this book, my teaching through these seven principles helped more than five hundred thousand Christ followers redeem their time, and I'm confident the same can be true for you.

While these principles will help you see that the key to redeeming your time is found in our Redeemer, that is far from the only place you will see them at work. Each chapter is chock-full of science and stories that illustrate the wisdom of Jesus's habits, including case studies from C. S. Lewis, Tamika Catchings, William Wilberforce, Dr. Martin Luther King Jr., Shay Cochrane, and Mister Rogers.

Practices

After introducing each timeless principle, I will recommend a handful of practices to help you apply the principle in our modern context.

Each practice was developed through years of research, nearly one hundred podcast interviews with some of the world's most productive Christ followers, and *tons* of personal experimentation. The practices I've shared aren't things I started experimenting with last week; these are the practices I and others have stuck with for *years* as a means of redeeming our time.

But I want to make one thing clear: while the principles in this book find their root in Scripture, the practices do not. The practices are simply my opinion about how to best live out the biblical principles in our modern context. Because of that, some of these practices may not work for you. I'm confident *many* of them will, but I'd be naive to think they *all* will. Results may vary depending on your current work and life circumstances.

On that note, let me offer two tips. First, *feel free to skip practices you don't find helpful.* If you start reading a practice and find that you already "get it" or that it is too tactical for your taste, by all means, please skip ahead. Each chapter has two to nine practices, for a total of thirty-two in this book. That's *a lot* of practical opportunities to redeem your time. I'm confident that even if you adopt only one of the thirty-two practices, this book will have been well worth your time.

Second, *beware of implementing too many practices at once.* Many time-management books take the approach of "You have to do it all and do it now or it won't work." That's not my approach here. It's taken me *more than a decade* to work these practices into my life. You shouldn't expect to adopt them all in a month. While you might read this book in a couple of days, a week, or a month, my hope is that it will be a book you come back to over and over again for years to revisit principles and pick up new practices for redeeming your time.

MY PROMISE TO YOU

You know what the most shockingly consistent thing was in those forty-plus time-management books I read? Nearly every author promised that his or her method to solving our time-management problems is *easy.* I get it—that promise is how you sell books. There's just one problem: *it's not true.* Not even close. You know how I know? Because the Bible tells me so. Sin messed everything up, ensuring we will all die with unfinished symphonies. Genesis 3:17 says that "cursed is the ground" we walk on; "painful" is our "toil." After the Fall, work is still good, work is still worship, but work—whether at the office or at home—is *hard.* So is redeeming our time.

But we choose to redeem our time not *despite* it being hard but precisely *because* it is hard. Oftentimes, saying something is hard is just another way of saying it's worth doing. So here's my promise to you: the work of redeeming your time *will not* be easy, but it *will* be worth it. Why? Because at the end of this road is a more Christlike version of yourself: purposeful, present, and *wildly* productive on his behalf. Are you up for the challenge? Then let's begin!

REDEEMING YOUR TIME

CHAPTER 1

START WITH THE WORD

To redeem our time in the model of our Redeemer, we must first know the
Author of time, his purposes for the world, and what he has called us to do
with the time he has given us.

William Wilberforce was *easily* one of the most productive
people of all time. He was elected to the British Parliament at the insanely young age of twenty-one.[1] At a single
point in time, he held official roles with sixty-nine different social-
reform groups in Great Britain.[2] Oh yeah, and he was chiefly responsible for abolishing the slave trade throughout the British Empire. In
the words of one of Wilberforce's many biographers, "It's difficult to
escape the verdict that William Wilberforce was simply the greatest
social reformer in the history of the world."[3]

But Wilberforce wasn't always productive to such noble ends.
For his first five years in Parliament, his ambition was largely for the
acquisition of more power and wealth. But at the age of twenty-six,
the boy-king surrendered himself to the lordship of King Jesus, ushering in what he called the "Great Change" of his life.[4]

That great change in his soul almost led to a dramatic change in
his work. After his conversion, Wilberforce sought out career advice
from his friend John Newton, the minister famous for writing the
hymn "Amazing Grace." Wilberforce fully expected Newton to advise
him to drop out of Parliament so he could "live now for God."[5] But
"Newton didn't tell him what he had expected—that to follow God
he would have to leave politics. On the contrary, Newton encouraged Wilberforce to stay where he was, saying that God could use
him there. Most others in Newton's place would likely have insisted

that Wilberforce pull away from the very place where his salt and light were most needed. How good that Newton did not."[6] Indeed. If Wilberforce's "Great Change" had led to a great change in his work, where would the world be today? Certainly much further from God's kingdom being "on earth as it is in heaven" (Matthew 6:10).

But while Wilberforce's "Great Change" didn't lead to a change in *what* he did vocationally, his salvation *did* lead to two dramatic changes in *how* he worked in Parliament. First, the object of his work changed from the raw pursuit of wealth and power to what he called his "great object":[7] the abolition of the slave trade. Second, and most relevant to the topic of this book, post-conversion Wilberforce dramatically changed how he managed his time.

In the days and weeks following his conversion experience, Wilberforce grieved over how he had spent his first twenty-six years on earth. One of his journal entries from this time reads, "I condemned myself for having wasted my precious time, and opportunities, and talents."[8] But Wilberforce didn't grieve long, for he was determined to redeem whatever time he had left to work on behalf of God's agenda rather than his own.

There was just one problem: Wilberforce was "an undisciplined mess" and "constitutionally weak . . . with regard to self-discipline"[9] (an encouraging note if you're starting this book believing that self-discipline and good time-management habits can't be learned). Wilberforce knew he had to overcome these challenges in order to partner most fully with God on his mission in the world. In his journal, Wilberforce resolved that this was his aspiration: "to endeavour from this moment to amend my plan for time. I hope to live more than heretofore to God's glory and my fellow-creatures' good."[10]

And amend his plan for time he did. Wilberforce's newfound faith manifested itself in *incredibly* practical ways. He journaled instructions to himself, such as "Go to bed at eleven and wake at six," to ensure he was getting adequate sleep.[11] He began carrying ink, quill, and paper in his pockets so he would never lose track of an idea while walking through London.[12] And he ruthlessly sought out solitude as his celebrity status began to rise, knowing how critical it was to make space to pray and think about what precisely he should be spending his time on. These practical time-management tactics contributed to Wilberforce's transformation from "an undisciplined mess" to one of the most productive people who has ever lived.

And he wasn't just productive in Parliament. He was also a prolific writer. In 1797, in the middle of his fight against slavery, Wilberforce published the first of three significant books, a work of theology titled *A Practical View of Christianity*. Ironically, the book really wasn't "practical" at all, at least not in the way we typically think of that word. There were no five-step processes. There were no checklists or discussion questions at the end of each chapter. There was just Wilberforce expounding upon the core tenets of the gospel that led to such dramatic changes in his life, work, and habits for managing time.

The subject of Wilberforce's first book is surprising, to say the least. At the time, Wilberforce's celebrity was not insignificant. While he had yet to achieve his "great object" of abolishing the slave trade, he had become widely known for his underdog fight against slavery's powerful proponents. Undoubtedly, the British people were interested in anything Wilberforce would have to say in his first published work. So why not focus the book on the evils of slavery or a manifesto on how Christians could engage practically to shape culture? I think it's because Wilberforce knew this: *theology always shapes our practices*.

Like William Wilberforce, the book you hold in your hands is *extremely* practical. But it will start out as one of the most theological. Why? Because, as Wilberforce understood, our persistent problems with time management are rooted in something much deeper than the wrong to-do-list systems or daily planners. Our problems are rooted in misconceptions of what we believe about work, time, and the role we have to play in God's mission in the world.

FIVE BIBLICAL TRUTHS ABOUT TIME AND PRODUCTIVITY

There's an ancient proverb that says, "If you want to know what water is, the fish is the last thing to ask."[13] Just as fish can't define what they're swimming in, neither can we. We swim in time, so to understand what time is, we must look outside ourselves for answers. In the words of Os Guinness, "If we are to master time, we must come to know the author of time, the meaning of time, and come to know the part he calls us to play in his grand story."[14]

Who is the author of time? God himself, of course. Genesis 1 shows God, a timeless being, creating the first day and time itself. Revelation 22:13 tells us that God is "the Alpha and the Omega, the First and the Last, the Beginning and the End." In short, God is the author and creator of the bookends of time.

In the 1970s, a Harvard professor found that the number one predictor of effectiveness in one's career is having a "long time perspective."[15] Stephen Covey popularized this idea in *The 7 Habits of Highly Effective People* by imploring readers to "begin with the end in mind."[16] As we've just seen, God is the keeper of the ultimate "long time perspective"—the creator of "the end" we are all to keep in mind. Thus, if our aim is to redeem our time, it is imperative that we start with his Word. Let's take a look at five things Scripture has to say about time and our role in it.

Truth #1: Our Longing for Timelessness Is Good and God Given

Deep in our bones, we know that we were created to live forever. It's why we are drawn to stories in which death is ultimately a lie. We love *The Lord of the Rings* because we know that everything sad *should* come untrue. We love *Tangled* because we believe there *should* be magical hair that can heal any wound. We love *Frozen* because we feel we *should* live in a world where magical snowmen never die.*

But we don't just long to *live* forever—we also long to *be productive* forever. Now, we don't feel like this every day. Sin has made work and our efforts to be productive difficult. But something in our souls (and in God's Word) tells us that work was meant to be *very* good. You see this in Genesis 2:15: "The LORD God took the man and put him in the Garden of Eden to work it and take care of it." The Hebrew word for "work" here is *avodah*, which is also translated to mean "worship" in our Bibles.[17] Work existed pre-sin. Work was good. Work was *more* than good—work was *worship*.

> *Work existed pre-sin. Work was good. Work was more than good—work was worship.*

I think we all have caught glimpses of what work must have been like prior to the Fall. You deliver a killer sales pitch and feel completely in your element. You finish writing a great chapter and can't wait to share it with your spouse. You hammer the last nail into a table and step back and admire your creation with healthy pride. These moments are what we might call feeling God's pleasure in our work.† If you've experienced even just one of these moments, you know what it feels like to want work like that to last forever. You don't want it to end, because you know deep in your soul that you were put on this earth to *do* something—to "make a mark" toward some end. Playwright Arthur Miller said it best in *Death of a Salesman* when he wrote that

---

* Apologies in advance for the number of analogies from Disney princess movies. I'm writing this when our girls are six, four, and one, so those movies are basically all I'm watching these days.

† Curious to learn more about what this looks like? Check out chapter 11 of my previous book, *Master of One: Find and Focus on the Work You Were Created to Do.*

our desire "to leave a thumbprint somewhere on the world" is a "need greater than hunger or sex or thirst. . . . A need for immortality, and by admitting it, the knowing that one has carefully inscribed one's name on a cake of ice on a hot July day."[18]

I know some Christians believe that this longing for timelessness is rooted in pride. I certainly used to think that. But the more I study Scripture, the more I'm convinced that this desire to live and be productive forever was designed by God himself. Ecclesiastes 3:11 makes this crystal clear, saying that God has "set eternity in the human heart." Jen Wilkin said it this way: "God . . . has given time-bound humans a longing for timelessness."[19]

This is one of the main themes of the musical *Hamilton.** Summarizing what he wants out of life, Alexander says, "I wanna build something that's gonna outlive me."[20] But Alexander's wife, Eliza, can't understand her husband's need for immortality. She urges her husband to "just stay alive—that would be enough."[21]

But we all know that's *not* enough. We *know* that we weren't created to just stay alive and get through this life. Something in our God-designed DNA tells us that we were made for something more. To be human is to work with time that our minds tell us is finite but that our souls assure us *shouldn't* be finite. So why *is* time finite?

Truth #2: Sin Has Ensured We Will All Die with Unfinished Symphonies

When sin entered the world, death was ushered in alongside it (see Genesis 3; 1 Corinthians 15:21). Human beings, who were created to be immortal, became mortal. Work, which was created to be good, became difficult. Time, which was created to be infinite, became finite.

---

*If you thought my *Hamilton* references would stop by now, think again. There are *lots* of *Hamilton* "Easter eggs" in this book for you super fans. Happy hunting!

In short, sin has ensured that nobody will ever finish the work he or she envisions completing in a lifetime. Karl Rahner, an influential Catholic theologian, put it like this: "In the torment of the insufficiency of everything attainable, we learn that ultimately in this world there is no finished symphony."[22]

Haunting, depressing, and so true. We will all die with unfinished symphonies. Our to-do lists will never be completed. There will always be a gap between what we can imagine accomplishing in this life and what we actually get done. Even Wilberforce "went to the grave sincerely and deeply regretting that he hadn't done much more."[23] Are you kidding me? If the man who virtually ended slavery felt he had unfinished symphonies, you can guarantee you and I will too.

> *There will always be a gap between what we can*
> *imagine accomplishing in this life and what we actually*
> *get done. We will all die with unfinished symphonies.*

Quite the uplifting start to this book, huh? Stick with me. I promise that *great* hope is right around the corner, but we have to start here because our grieving over the finiteness of time is the clue that gets us to that hope. In the words of one of Wilberforce's biographers, Eric Metaxas, "No human impulse is more fundamental than our desire to transcend time, and none argues better that time is not the medium for which we are finally meant."[24] C. S. Lewis put it this way: "If I find in myself a desire which no experience in this world can satisfy, the most probable explanation is that I was made for another world."[25]

So, if we long to accomplish more than what sin will allow us to in one lifetime, it's logical to assume that we were made for a different, timeless story. And that is precisely what the Christian narrative is all about—that while it may appear that we will all die with unfinished symphonies, ultimately this is just an illusion, as "God is able to bring eternal results from our time-bound efforts."[26]

Truth #3: God Will Finish the Work We Leave Unfinished

Okay, so God created us to live forever, but sin has broken creation and made us mortal, time bound, and finite. Where's the hope? Our hope is found in Jesus Christ's walking out of the tomb that first Easter morning with a redeemed body that could not be destroyed again. The Resurrection was the emphatic "end of 'nevermore.'"[27] It was Jesus's way of declaring that our longing for immortality has been right all along and that through him, we too can experience eternal life.

The Resurrection was the emphatic "end of 'nevermore.'"

But Easter wasn't just the beginning of eternal *life*—it also marked the inauguration of God's eternal *kingdom*. Look at the Gospels: Jesus *hardly ever* talked about the gospel of individual salvation, focusing the majority of his teaching on what he called the "gospel of the kingdom" (Matthew 24:14). The point? Easter isn't just good news for our *souls*. It's good news for the *world*.

What does this have to do with time management? It helps us make sense of where time is *going*. The Christian story is that God created us to live and work with him in a perfect garden. Sin messed everything up, but God promised to send a King to set everything right. With his defeat of death on Easter, Jesus proved emphatically that he is that promised King. And everything from that moment to the end of Revelation is about the building of God's kingdom until Jesus returns to finish what he started at the Resurrection and make "*all* things new" (Revelation 21:5, ESV).

So, if Jesus is coming back to finish his kingdom, why does it matter what you and I do in the present? Why does it matter that we redeem our time today? Because God has invited us to co-labor with him to build for his eternal kingdom! That is what Paul was saying in 1 Corinthians 3:9 when he called us "God's fellow workers" (ESV). And if you think about it, that is how God has been working since the beginning. In Genesis, God created a lot in six days, but what's equally remarkable is what he did *not* create. The first few days of creation was God setting up a canvas. The sixth day was when he passed the baton of creation to us—his image bearers—and called us to *fill* that canvas [literally, to "fill the earth" (1:28)] with things that point to his glory.

The same thing happened Easter morning. Jesus inaugurated his kingdom with the Resurrection, but he left the work of building for that kingdom to us until he returns to finish the work once and for all. N. T. Wright, whom *Newsweek* has called "the world's leading New Testament scholar,"[28] put it this way: "God's kingdom, inaugurated through Jesus, is all about restoring creation the way it was meant to be. *God always wanted to work in his world through loyal human beings.*"[29]

William Wilberforce is a perfect picture of this.* Slavery has no place in God's kingdom, but God used Wilberforce and others to fight against that remnant of sin, bringing us a few steps closer to God's kingdom. As the former president of Wilberforce University pointed out, "Wilberforce's life allows us to witness that God has not finished his creative work."[30]

Our work matters *today* because it is a means of glorifying God and loving our neighbors as ourselves (see Matthew 22:39). But our work also matters for *eternity* because God can use it to build his kingdom. And because God alone will finish that work and ultimately bring heaven to earth, we can embrace this freeing truth today: *God doesn't need you or me to finish our to-do lists.* If the things on our to-do lists are on *God's* to-do list, he will complete them with or without us.

God doesn't need you or me to finish our to-do lists. If the things on our to-do lists are on God's to-do list, he will complete them with or without us.

---

* By the way, if you want to read more about Wilberforce's remarkable story, check out my devotional series based on his life. You'll find the link at JordanRaynor .com/RYT.

God didn't need Moses specifically to lead the Israelites into the Promised Land, so he finished that work through Joshua. God didn't need David specifically to build the temple, so he finished that work through Solomon. If I die tomorrow and the Lord wants my work to continue, he will find someone else to do the job or he will simply finish my work when he brings heaven to earth.

God is directing a master narrative for the world, and I am just one of billions of actors in that story. In his great grace and wisdom, he has given me exactly as much time as I need to participate in that grand drama and work toward his kingdom. Not a moment more. Not a moment less. In the words of Job, "A person's days are determined; you have decreed the number of his months and have set limits he cannot exceed" (Job 14:5). Thank God for those limits that ensure that he alone will get the glory for finishing the work we leave unfinished. As Jen Wilkin wrote, "Thanks be to God for the limit of time, by which we are bound and he is not."[31]

Truth #4: The Gospel Is Our Source of Rest and Ambition

As we've seen, God doesn't need us to be productive, but *we* often need *ourselves* to be productive in order to feel a sense of self-worth. There is certainly proper ambition for productivity, and we will get to that in just a moment, but before we go any further, we have to stop and let this truth sink in: *the gospel frees us from the* need *to be productive.*

The good news of the gospel is that "while we were still sinners, Christ died for us" (Romans 5:8) and invited us to work for and live in his kingdom forever. And because we did nothing to *earn* his grace, there is nothing we can do to *lose* it. No matter how productive you are in this life, your status as an adopted child of God will never ever change. In the words of the great preacher Martyn Lloyd-Jones, "A Christian *is* something before he does anything."[32]

Every night as I put our girls to bed, I ask them, "Do you know I love you no matter how many good things you do?" They nod their heads. "Do you know I love you no matter how many bad things you do?" They nod again. Then I ask, "Who else loves you like that?" and they always reply, "Jesus." Or as Kate, my four-year-old stickler for theology, says, "God the Father, Jesus, and the Holy Spirit."

You and I need to hear those same words applied to our efforts to redeem our time. God loves us no matter how productive or unproductive we are in this life. And ironically, it's that truth that leads us to be wildly productive. Why? Because working to earn someone's favor is exhausting, but working in response to unconditional favor is intoxicating. For Christians, the key to being wildly productive is realizing that we don't *need* to be productive.[33] Once we realize that God accepts us no matter how many good things we do, we *want* to be productive for his agenda as a loving act of worship.

> *Working to earn someone's favor is exhausting, but working in response to unconditional favor is intoxicating.*

So, what *is* his agenda? What does Scripture tell us God wants us doing with the time he has given us? The apostle Paul wrote, "We are his workmanship, created in Christ Jesus for good works, which God prepared beforehand, that we should walk in them" (Ephesians 2:10, ESV). Jesus said, "Let your light shine before others, so that they may see your good works and give glory to your Father who is in heaven" (Matthew 5:16, ESV). In other words, the very purpose of our lives—the reason we were created and saved—was to do good works that advance God's kingdom and glorify him in the process.

Now, I can guess what you're thinking: *But, Jordan, when Jesus and Paul said "good works," they were talking about giving money to the poor, not writing an elegant line of code, right?* Wrong. Of course "good works" implies charitable and evangelical things, but the meaning of *ergon* (the Greek word that translates to "good works" in these verses) is *much* broader. The word is used to connote "work, task, [and] employment."[34]

Remember, work was part of God's perfect world prior to the Fall, and Jesus reaffirmed the goodness of what many would deem secular work by spending the vast majority of his adult life working as a carpenter. So why *shouldn't* we expect plain old good work to be central to God's call on our lives?

As we've seen, work—*good* work—is a means of advancing God's kingdom and glorifying him. If that's so, then the gospel of the kingdom should lead us to be *incredibly* ambitious for our work today. Pastor John Piper went as far as saying that "aimless, unproductive Christians contradict the creative, purposeful, powerful, merciful God we love."[35]

Furthermore, while Scripture tells us that our relative productivity has no bearing on our *status* as adopted children of God, it makes equally clear that we all will have different *rewards* in the kingdom based on how we steward our time in this life. The parable of the talents makes this clear (see Matthew 25:14–30), as does much of 1 Corinthians and Ephesians 6:8, which says, "The Lord will reward each one for whatever good they do."

All of this should lead to a burning desire to steward our time well—not because we *need* to be productive, but because the gospel *compels* us to be. Part of our response to the gospel—to our security as "dearly loved children" (Ephesians 5:1) of God—is to redeem our time, stewarding every hour as wisely as we can for the good of others, the advancement of the kingdom, and God's great glory.

The question now is straightforward: Where can we look for practical wisdom as to how to redeem our time? The answer is to God's Word generally, but more specifically to the life of Christ—the eternal God who became a time-bound human being.

START WITH THE WORD

Truth #5: We Can Know How God Would Manage His Time

When the Author of time "became flesh" (John 1:14), he became *fully* human, meaning that he experienced the same day-to-day challenges other mortals faced. He had a business to run, a mother and father to care for, hunger to manage, and the need for sleep. Oh yeah, and he faced the same twenty-four-hour time constraint as every other human being. As pastor Timothy Keller explained, "Besides being vulnerable, subject to injury and death, [Jesus] had the limitations of being confined to one place in time and space."[36] Like us, Jesus had a finite amount of time to finish the work the Father gave him to do (see 17:4).

All throughout the Gospels, you see that Jesus was painfully aware that the clock was ticking. In John 9:4, he said, "As long as it is day, we must do the works of him who sent me. Night is coming, when no one can work."

Okay, Jordan, Jesus had a finite amount of time on earth. But surely the demands on his time in the first century can't compare to what we experience today, can they? Absolutely. As we'll see throughout this book, Jesus had to deal with interruptions, constant noise, and many of the other time-management challenges we struggle with today. As pastor Kevin DeYoung has written, "If Jesus were alive today, he'd get more e-mails than any of us. He'd have people calling his cell all the time. He'd have a zillion requests for interviews, television appearances, and conference gigs. Jesus did not float above the fray, untouched by the pressures of normal human existence."[37]

But, Jordan, do the Gospels really have anything to say about how Jesus spent his time on earth? Now we're getting somewhere! Yes, they do—quite a bit, in fact. But to see it, we must adjust the lens through which we read them.

One of my favorite pastors and writers, John Mark Comer, has written extensively about the fact that modern Christians read the

Gospels almost exclusively looking for *theology* and *ethics*. And while Matthew, Mark, Luke, and John certainly have a lot to say about theology and ethics, we must remember that their narratives are also *biographies* of the life of Christ. But as Comer explained, "*Very few followers of Jesus read the four Gospels that way. We read them as cute sermon illustrations or allegorical pick-me-ups or theological gold mines. Again, not bad, but we often miss the proverbial forest for the trees. They are biographies.*"[38]

When you read a biography, "you don't just look at what [the person] *said* or *did;* you look at *how* he or she *lived the details of day-to-day life.* If you're smart, you copy those details, make the individual's habits your habits; his or her routine, your routine; his or her values, your values in the hope that it will foster a similar kind of result in your own more ordinary life."[39]

The Gospels are our opportunity to see not just what Jesus said or what he did but *how he walked,* so that we can walk and manage our time as he did. In the words of the apostle John, "Whoever says he abides in [Christ] ought to walk in the same way in which he walked" (1 John 2:6, ESV). The biographies of the Gospels ensure that we don't have to wonder how Jesus walked. In the words of author Emily P. Freeman, "We don't have to wonder what God would do if he were a person. He is a person, and here is what he did."[40]

The Gospels are our opportunity to see not just what Jesus said or what he did but how he walked, so that we can walk and manage our time as he did.

Okay, then how did Jesus walk? How did he manage his time? Those are the questions we will explore throughout the remainder of this book as we examine seven time-management principles from the life of Christ and map them to corresponding practices that can help us live out those principles in the twenty-first century.

Perhaps the most obvious principle is this: Jesus's efforts to redeem his time started with the Word in both a theological sense and a practical one. Theologically, Jesus obviously knew the biblical truths about time we have been exploring in this chapter. Starting with the Word in this theological sense had to shape his perspective on time while he was on earth. But Jesus also started with the Word in a practical, day-to-day sense, frequently breaking away from the crowds and his disciples to spend time alone with his Father.

If you and I are to make the most of our time, we too must start with the Word, which brings us to our first principle in this book.

> PRINCIPLE #1
> START WITH THE WORD
>
> To redeem our time in the model of our Redeemer, we must first know the Author of time, his purposes for the world, and what he has called us to do with the time he has given us.

How do we live out this principle on a day-to-day basis? Allow me to suggest two simple but crucial practices.

PRACTICE 1: SPEND TIME WITH THE AUTHOR OF TIME

It's not enough to read the principle above just once. To redeem our time for God's purposes, we need to develop the habit of communing with him through the study of his Word on a daily basis.

Yes, the first practice I'm recommending in this supposedly revolutionary book on time management is to have a "quiet time." I know.

How novel. But if we are going to redeem our time, we've got to start where our Redeemer started. And as the Gospels make clear, Jesus prioritized time with his Father above everything else, including sleep (see Mark 1:35; Luke 6:12).

Why is this practice so important? Four reasons.

First and most obvious, time in the Word is how we commune with God. We spend time in the Scriptures not to get something from God but to "get God" himself. *He* is the prize.

Second, apart from him, we can do *nothing*. You picked up this book because you want to be purposeful, present, and productive. But Jesus stated clearly that we can do nothing of eternal significance without being connected to him: "I am the vine; you are the branches. If you remain in me and I in you, you will bear much fruit; apart from me you can do nothing" (John 15:5). I love how bluntly author Matt Perman put it: "To live your life without God is the most unproductive thing you can do."[41]

Third, time in Scripture gives us more time. For those of you thinking, *Jordan, I'm just too busy for a daily quiet time,* read what Proverbs 9:10–11 has to say: "The fear of the LORD is the beginning of wisdom, and knowledge of the Holy One is understanding. For through wisdom your days will be many, and years will be added to your life." Proverbs 10:27 says the same thing: "The fear of the LORD adds length to life, but the years of the wicked are cut short." Does time in God's Word *literally* extend our lives? That question is way above my pay grade. But what's impossible to dispute is that immersing ourselves in the wisdom of Scripture will help us make wiser use of our time toward God's purposes. And that, in effect, acts as a force multiplier to the fixed amount of time we have been given.

Finally, time in the Word is the keystone habit that makes every other time-management practice easier or more effective. In his book *The Power of Habit,* Charles Duhigg popularized the idea of keystone habits, which "have the power to start a chain reaction, changing other habits" in our lives.[42] According to Duhigg's research, "Keystone habits start a process that, over time, transforms everything."⁴³ *That* is the power of daily steeping ourselves in Scripture.

Time in the Word is the keystone habit that makes every other time-management practice easier or more effective.

Spending time in God's Word reminds us of the importance of ensuring that our yes is yes (see chapter 2), as doing so is a means of preserving the reputation of Christ followers and the gospel. Time in Scripture guarantees that we regularly "dissent from the kingdom of noise" (see chapter 3) so we can hear and listen to God's voice. The Word helps us define what really matters in our lives and our work (see chapter 4) by renewing our minds with eternal perspective. Focusing intensely and singularly on Scripture every day helps us work out our "focus muscles," which are critical to cultivating depth at work and home (see chapter 5). Committing to time in the Word each day forces us to get enough rest so we don't fall asleep on top of our Bibles (see chapter 6). And finally, daily time in the Word is one way you can "acknowledge him" so that "he will make straight your paths" (Proverbs 3:6, ESV) as you plan your days and budget your time (see chapter 7).

So, what does this first practice actually look like? It's not rocket science, and if you're already in the habit of spending time each day in the Word, feel free to skip ahead to practice 2. But if time in Scripture is still a struggle for you, here are some practical tips.

First, you have to choose *when* you can be in God's Word on a consistent basis. For me that's first thing in the morning. As you'll see in chapter 7, my daily Time Budget starts with time in the Word every morning from five to six. That's the time when I am least likely to be interrupted. It's also when I am at my best mentally.

But you might *not* be at your best at five in the morning. Although most people are morning larks, a significant percentage of people are biologically wired to be night owls. If you're a night owl, five o'clock in the morning probably isn't the best time to engage meaningfully with God's Word. In the Gospels, we see Jesus spending time with his Father both early in the morning (see Mark 1:35) and late at night (see Luke 6:12). Whatever works for you works. What's important is that you do it.

Once you've nailed down *when* you will be in the Word each day, you'll need a plan for *what* you will do with that time. Personally, I love Martin Luther's method of studying the Bible. It begins by reading a passage of Scripture (I usually read one chapter along with a commentary by Timothy Keller or N. T. Wright). Then we respond to the text by writing out:

1. Instruction (what the passage is commanding you to do)
2. Praise (what the passage leads you to praise God for)
3. Confession (where you have fallen short of the passage's instruction)
4. Petition (for God's grace in helping you live out the commands of the passage)[44]

Time in God's Word can look a hundred different ways. Luther's way is just one of many. If you find it helpful, give it a shot.

God's Word is the source of all wisdom. How do you get wisdom? Solomon's answer to that question in Proverbs 4 is *so* good. The wisest man who ever lived spent the first nine verses of the chapter urging his reader to pursue godly wisdom at all cost. You can almost hear his reader saying, "Okay, yes! I need God's wisdom. Where do I start? What are the three steps to getting it?" Solomon replied, "The beginning of wisdom is this: Get wisdom" (verse 7, ESV). Essentially, Solomon said, "Just get it!" Pick a time, pick a method, and *just do it.*

But, Jordan, you don't understand how busy I am. There's no way I can add something new to my schedule! Trust me, I get it. Remember how crazy my life is right now? *Three* kids six and under. In the words of President Clinton, "I feel your pain."[45] But look at the biographies of

START WITH THE WORD   19

Jesus in the Gospels: the *busier* Jesus got, the *more* time he spent with his Father. We must do the same. Martin Luther once said, "I have so much to do today, I'll need to spend another hour on my knees."[46] That's the sentiment. The busier we get (and let's face it: we're *all* busy), the more we need the wisdom of God to redeem our time for his purposes.

But, Jordan, I've done "quiet times" before and gotten nothing out of it. Me too—present tense. There are some days that I just sit with a passage and get nowhere. But remember, this is a *relationship,* and "relational time is wildly inefficient."[47] If you've had young kids, you know what I'm talking about. About 80 percent of the conversations I have with my four-year-old are total nonsense, but I put in the effort to get to the 20 percent that are pure gold. Regardless of the proportions, *all* relational time—including our time with the Lord—can feel inefficient at certain moments. But that's no excuse not to engage. John Mark Comer nailed it: "If you love God the Father and want a living, thriving relationship with him . . . then you need to carve out time to be alone with him. Full stop."[48]

But, Jordan, suggesting a daily quiet time sounds so legalistic. I hear you. Like many good things, we can easily become legalistic about personal quiet times. *Please* don't think I'm saying that you have to have daily devotions to experience God's favor. That is completely contrary to the gospel. *But* prioritizing daily time with the Author of time is one of the primary ways we can demonstrate our devotion to the Lord. And *nothing* will have a greater impact on our efforts to be purposeful, present, and productive toward his aims.

PRACTICE 2: PRAY WHAT YOU KNOW

When Phil Knight was starting Nike, the challenges were immense. In addition to the considerable hurdles that come standard with any entrepreneurial journey, Knight had to deal with dishonest partners, unjust lawsuits, the loss of key team members—the works. In his inimitable autobiography, *Shoe Dog,* Knight explained how he relieved the pressure at the end of each day: "I'd retreat to my recliner, where I'd administer the nightly self-catechism."[49] There in his living room, Knight would not dwell on what *might* happen to him and his business. Rather, he focused his thoughts on a single question: "What do I *know*?" Only by articulating what he *knew* to be true was he able to obtain calm in the everyday chaos.

As you and I seek to redeem our time, we would be wise to do the same, preaching to ourselves through prayer the biblical truths we've explored in this chapter. To that end, allow me to suggest that you pray what you now know regarding time and your role in it—daily, weekly, at whatever cadence feels right to you. Of course, you can use whatever words you'd like, but you're also free to borrow my own prayer:

Lord, thank you that my longing for timelessness is not a mirage. Thank you for setting eternity inside my heart (see Ecclesiastes 3:11).

I humbly recognize that I will die with unfinished symphonies but that if my work is aligned with your will, *you* will finish my work in your time. As John the Baptist said, "I am not the Christ" (John 1:20, ESV), and therefore I don't need to complete my to-do list in order for your purposes to prevail (see Proverbs 19:21).

Father, thank you that through Jesus I can never lose my status as your adopted child; thus, I have no *need* to be productive. But I graciously accept your invitation to do as many good works as I can for your glory, the good of others, and the advancement of your kingdom.

Proverbs 16:3 says, "Commit to the LORD whatever you do, and he will establish your plans." Lord, I commit my day and my to-do list to you. Establish my plans in accordance with your will. Help me to be purposeful, present, and wildly productive for your purposes today.

But regardless of how productive I am, I will *know* that you love me. May the security of your love make me both peaceful and ambitious to do your will today. Amen.*

COLLECTING THE PUZZLE PIECES

To extend the puzzle analogy from the introduction, the cornerstone of Christ is the corner *piece* of the puzzle to redeeming your time. As Mr. Beaver said about Aslan the Christlike lion, "Once he's with us, then we can begin doing things."⁵⁰ But before we ensure we are focusing our time on doing the "right things," it is critical that we extract everything we could be doing from our minds and put those items into a trusted external system. That's the critical puzzle piece we will pick up in the next chapter. Oh, and if you're still wondering when this book is going to get practical, buckle up. Chapter 2 is the most practical in the entire book.

*Want to keep this "productivity prayer" handy? There's a link to print out a copy at JordanRaynor.com/RYT.

CHAPTER 2

LET YOUR YES BE YES

To redeem our time in the model of our Redeemer, we must ensure that
our yes is yes from the smallest to the biggest commitments we make.

When Mozart was a young man living at home with his father, Leopold, he enjoyed playing a little trick on his old man. After a night out in Vienna with his friends, Mozart would return home to find his father fast asleep. Mozart would then sit down at the family's piano and loudly play a rising scale of notes, only to stop one note short of completing the scale. Satisfied with the knowledge of what would inevitably come next, Mozart would go to bed.

As Mozart was falling asleep, Leopold would invariably begin to wake with the unfinished scale tossing and turning in his head. He couldn't bear the lack of resolution. Eventually, Leopold would drag himself out of bed, make his way to the piano, and play the last note. Only then could he go back to sleep.[1]

You've likely experienced something similar. You're driving down the road when a song you loathe starts to play. You turn the song off, but now you can't seem to get the terrible tune out of your head. Like Mozart's father, the unfinished song plays on in your mind long after the music stops playing.

Why is it that the *worst* songs are some of the hardest to get out of our heads? Is it because they're uniquely catchy? That might be part of it. But there's actually a scientific answer to this question. The answer is found in what psychologists call the Zeigarnik effect, in which "uncompleted tasks"—or, in this case, unfinished songs—"tend to pop into one's mind" over and over again.[2] Dr. Roy Baumeister, one of the world's leading social psychologists, explained:

> A good way to appreciate the Zeigarnik effect is to listen to a randomly chosen song and shut it off halfway through. The song is then likely to run through your mind on its own, at odd intervals. . . . As if to keep reminding you that there is a job to be done, the mind keeps inserting bits of the song into your stream of thought. . . . And that's why this kind of ear worm is so often an awful tune rather than a pleasant one. We're more likely to turn off the bad one in midsong, so it's the one that returns to haunt us.[3]

Of course, an "ear worm" created by an unfinished song doesn't have much of an impact on our efforts to redeem our time. But the ones caused by unexternalized tasks and commitments do—*a lot*—contributing greatly to our anxiety and ability to focus at work and at home.

To prove this, Dr. Baumeister and his colleagues at Florida State University* conducted an experiment in which all participants were asked to think about an important project that was on their minds. One group of participants was given no further instructions, while another group was asked to write down specific tasks they needed to do related to the project. They weren't asked to *complete* those tasks but were just supposed to make a plan for what exactly they needed to do at some point in the future.

After the groups received their instructions, they moved on to what appeared to be a separate experiment. Participants were then asked to read the first ten pages of a novel. Upon completion, Baumeister's team asked the participants a series of questions to gauge

*Go Noles!

how much their minds were distracted by their looming projects. In other words, the researchers were trying to discern which participants were able to stay the most focused on reading the novel.

The winners? The group who wrote down future tasks—by a long shot. "Even though they hadn't finished the task or made any palpable progress, the simple act of making a plan had cleared their minds and eliminated the Zeigarnik effect."[4] What's my point? Baumeister explained:

> If . . . you've got [a ton of] items on your to-do list, the Zeigarnik effect could leave you leaping from task to task, and it won't be sedated by vague good intentions. If you've got a memo that has to be read before a meeting Thursday morning, the unconscious wants to know exactly what needs to be done next, and under what circumstances. But once you make that plan . . . you can relax. You don't have to finish the job right away. You've still got [a ton of] things on the to-do list, but for the moment . . . the water is calm.[5]

A PRIMARY SOURCE OF OUR ANXIETY AND STRESS

The Zeigarnik effect is brought on by things we know we need to do but that we've failed to get out of our heads. David Allen, author of the mammoth bestseller *Getting Things Done,* calls these "open loops," which he defines as "anything pulling at your attention that doesn't belong where it is, the way it is."[6] That's a great definition, but given that open loops often represent commitments that we have made with ourselves or others, I prefer to define the term this way:

OPEN LOOP: anything personal or professional, big or small, urgent or distant, that you have any level of internal commitment to doing in the future

"Can you send me the PowerPoint before the call?"

"We should go to Hawaii for our twentieth anniversary!"

"I really need to convince the kids to get rid of these disgusting hermit crabs."

All of these statements represent open loops. Most of us have dozens, maybe *hundreds,* of open loops at any given time, and many of them are stored only in our minds. (You're likely thinking of a few right now.) That's a problem because God didn't design our brains to hold that much information. Allen explained:

> The short-term-memory part of your mind—the part that tends to hold all of [your open loops]—functions much like RAM (random-access memory) on a computer. Your conscious mind, like the computer screen, is a focusing tool, not a storage place. You can think about only two or three things at once. But the [open loops] are still being stored in the short-term-memory space. And as with RAM, there's limited capacity; there's only so much stuff you can store in there and still have that part of your brain function at a high level. Most people walk around with their RAM bursting at the seams.[7]

Of course, when our mental RAM is bursting with open loops, bad things happen—at least three things specifically. First, our open loops make it impossible for us to be fully present. World-renowned neuroscientist Dr. Daniel Levitin explained how:

> When we have something on our minds that is important—especially a To Do item—we're afraid we'll forget it, so our brain rehearses it, tossing it around and around in circles in something that cognitive psychologists actually refer to as the rehearsal loop, a network of brain regions that ties together

the frontal cortex just behind your eyeballs and the hippo-
campus in the center of your brain. . . . The problem is that
it works too well, keeping items in rehearsal until we attend
to them.[8]

Just one open loop is problematic for our ability to focus and be
fully present. Imagine dozens or hundreds of them! David Allen
explained further that when you know you need to do something but
"store it only in your head, there's a part of you that thinks you should
be doing that something *all the time.*"[9]

Sound familiar? If so, you can probably relate to this satirical news
flash from the *Onion:* "Local man Marshall Platt, 34, came tantaliz-
ingly close to kicking back and having a good time while attending
a friend's barbeque last night before remembering each and every
one of his professional and personal obligations, backyard sources
confirmed."[10] It's funny because it's true.

Here's the second problem that occurs when we fail to clear our
heads of open loops: from time to time, we are bound to drop the ball
and forget to do something. Why? Because trying to remember to-dos
"is like trying to catch fish with your bare hands."[11]

Need proof that we humans are terrible at remembering things?
Look at how common free trials have become in the past decade.
Companies such as Netflix and Spotify are so confident the majority
of people will forget to cancel their subscriptions that they're willing
to give their product away for free to get you to sign up.[*]

Here's the third and, in my opinion, most significant problem that
occurs when our "mental RAM" is bursting with open loops: having
an overwhelming number of open loops causes anxiety and stress. We
often attribute our stress to having "too much to do." But this can't
be true, because we *always* have too much to do, yet we don't *always*

---

[*]To be fair, the best companies also know that if their product is stellar, you'll stick
around because they're delivering great value. But my point still stands.

feel stressed and out of control. Maybe we feel that way *most* of the time, but not always. Ergo, the source of our stress must be rooted in something else.

Based on the research we've reviewed thus far, the true source of much of our anxiety and stress should be getting clearer: we're stressed because we fail to get open loops out of our brains, email inboxes, and other tools and into trusted, external systems.

Have you ever copied something to the clipboard on your computer, forgot to paste it, and then felt a tinge of anxiety? You felt like there was something you *should* be doing but hadn't, and that caused a smidge of stress. That's a tiny picture of the anxiety open loops can create with commitments that are exponentially more important than pasting a block of text.

And an open loop is nothing short of that: *a commitment* you have made to yourself or others. If I'm on a call with you and I say, "I'll send you a link to that book once we hop off," I have made a commitment to you. The *size* of the commitment is irrelevant. As the brain science makes clear, if I say I will do something and I fail to write that task down (and, of course, complete it sometime soon), my stress and anxiety will build. "Stress comes from unkept agreements with yourself" and others.[12]

Failing to collect, define, and do the things you say you're going to do is a much bigger deal than letting something slip through the cracks. In the words of Billy Joel, "It's a matter of trust."[13] And *because* it's a matter of trust, the stress that open loops cause should (and, in my experience, often do) affect Christ followers in significant and negative ways. Why? Because Jesus has told us, plain and simple, "Let your 'Yes' be 'Yes,' and your 'No,' 'No.' For whatever is more than these is from the evil one" (Matthew 5:37, NKJV). Yet again I bring Jen Wilkin to the plate to drive this point home:

> Do we do what we say we will do? Do we let our yes be yes and our no be no? . . .

Ultimately, every act of faithfulness toward others is an act of faithfulness toward God himself. Though others may make commitments they have little intention of keeping, the children of God strive to prove that their word is their bond. They do so not to win the trust or approval of others, but because they long to be like Christ. They long to hear with their ears, "Well done, good and faithful servant."[14]

The stress that open loops cause should affect Christ followers in significant and negative ways.

If we care deeply about walking how Jesus walked, we will care deeply about ensuring that our yes is yes. That brings us to the second biblical principle of this book.

PRINCIPLE #2
LET YOUR YES BE YES

To redeem our time in the model of our Redeemer, we must ensure that our yes is yes from the smallest to the biggest commitments we make.

Practicing this principle is one of *the keys* to alleviating our anxiety and stress. So, how do you do this? How do you ensure that your yes is yes when potential commitments come flying at you from a million different directions? The only solution is to get all your commitments—all your open loops—out of your head and into a trusted, external system.

A SOLUTION TO OUR ANXIETY AND STRESS

I know what you're thinking: *Jordan, the reason my open loops are in my head is that I don't have time to do them!*

I hear you, but remember what Dr. Baumeister's study showed: we don't have to actually close our open loops in order for our brains to let them go; we simply have to place them in trusted systems outside our minds. As Dr. Levitin explained, "Writing [open loops] down gives both implicit and explicit permission to [your brain] to let them go, to relax its neural circuits so that we can focus on something else."[15]

If you've ever made a to-do list when you were particularly overwhelmed, you've proven this point. Maybe it was a week before your wedding or the last time you were trying to wrap up work before going on vacation. There was *so* much to do that you simply *had* to make a to-do list. And do you remember how you felt after making that list? If you're like most people, you probably felt at least some sense of relief even though you hadn't completed a single thing on your list. The simple act of externalizing those open loops brought a sense of peace. If you want to feel like that every hour of every day, keep reading. I am promising nothing less in this chapter.

Of course, we even see this connection between unexternalized concerns and anxiety in Scripture. In Philippians 4:6–7, the apostle Paul wrote, "Do not be anxious about anything, but in every situation, by prayer and petition, with thanksgiving, present your requests to God. And the peace of God, which transcends all understanding, will guard your hearts and your minds in Christ Jesus." Paul was saying that part of the solution to our anxiety and stress is clearing our minds of concerns and requests, in this case through prayer. Matt Perman, a former member of John Piper's staff and the bestselling author of *What's Best Next*, made this observation about Paul's words in Philippians:

This passage also speaks of objectifying your concerns—getting them out of your mind—when it says to "let your requests be made known to God." . . . When [we speak] of getting . . . *every* incomplete out of your head rather than just some, [we are] echoing the same truth that the apostle Paul is calling attention to here.[16]

I promise that in just a moment we are going to get *hyper*-practical as I walk you through a proven process for externalizing your commitments. But first I want to address a concern I imagine some of you are having right now: *Jordan, why are we starting this book talking about to-do lists? This seems so small. Every other time-management book says, "Start with the end in mind," "Define your 'big three' tasks for the day and ignore everything else," or "Don't sweat the small stuff."*

Here's the problem: as we've already seen, your brain *can't help* but sweat the small stuff. Your God-designed mind makes no distinction between "small" and "big" stuff—all of it is *commitments* that will nag at your attention until you get them out of your brain and into a trusted system. You must deal with the stuff you've *already* committed to before you can prioritize your to-do list or dream about adding anything else to it. Doing otherwise is "like trying to swim in baggy clothing."[17]

Your brain can't help but sweat the small stuff.

In chapter 4, we are going to set big goals that help prioritize our to-do lists. But first we must collect all our open loops, creating a comprehensive inventory of the commitments we've already made. *Then* we can get to prioritizing and keeping our commitments—in other words, letting our yes be yes.

Before we jump into the first practice, I need to issue a warning: this chapter is by far the most practical in this book, as in "you might feel like you've gone back to school" practical. If that's not your cup of tea or you're confident you have a sufficient system to manage all your projects and to-dos, *please feel free to skip to chapter 3*. If you feel fully in control of your to-do list, you won't need the following practices to get the most out of the rest of this book. But if that's *not* you and you really want to solve this problem—if you really want an anxiety-reducing system for organizing all your open loops in a single place—this chapter will be *immensely* helpful. Are you ready? Let's dive in.

PRACTICE 1: CHOOSE A WORKFLOW

People are often asking me, "What to-do-list app should I use?" After clarifying how the person works, I almost always tell them, "Your biggest need isn't an app. What you need is a *workflow*." The right workflow allows you to do the following:

- Externalize and centralize all your open loops
- Organize a comprehensive library of your commitments
- Quickly re-center when chaos inevitably attacks your calendar
- Be fully present and focused because you're comfortable with what you're *not* doing
- Trust that you're working on the right things rather than hoping you are

Sound impossible? It did to me, too, until a decade ago. After my first company was acquired, I went to work as an executive at the acquiring company. My counterpart was a guy who became one of my closest friends, Erik Rapprich. It didn't take long for me to notice that Erik operated at a different level than anyone I had ever worked with before. In meetings, he was fully engaged, never checking his phone for fear that he was needed somewhere else. In emails, he was clear in his responses and never missed a needed reply. And most importantly, Erik never *ever* dropped a ball, even though he was managing dozens of complex projects at once. If Erik said he would do something, you could guarantee that it would get done. Every single time. His yes was *always* yes.

One day I asked Erik, "How do you do it? How are you able to operate at this level?" Erik smiled and said, "I'm about to change your life," to which I replied, "Then by all means, lead the way.'" That's when he introduced me to the workflow of *Getting Things Done*, the aforementioned book by David Allen, which, since its publication more than twenty years ago, has spawned a fanatical cult following.

Personally, I recognize that my ability to be hyper-productive is a gracious gift from God. But I credit *Getting Things Done* for being the dominant tool God has used to *deliver* that grace in my life.

Of course, having this great workflow is very satisfying to me, but more satisfying is the fact that *Getting Things Done* has helped ensure that the people around me trust me deeply. Just as I quickly learned to trust Erik to do whatever he said he was going to do, my family, friends, and team know that, more times than not, my yes will be yes. For the most part, I am a keeper of my word and thus a more accurate reflection of *the* Word.

To be clear, I am not perfect when it comes to managing my commitments. From time to time, I drop the ball, just like everybody else. But by the grace of God, those instances are exceedingly rare. By and large, I can be trusted to do what I say I'm going to do, and I almost never experience the stress that comes with feeling like I have too much on my plate.

Now to be clear, I am not a "*Getting Things Done* purist." Over the years, I have aggregated the best of *Getting Things Done* and other productivity workflows to develop my own unique system. In practices 2 through 5, I am going to take you step by step through my own personal workflow. If this workflow works for you, great. If not, I would encourage you to seek out another one, because as I hope you'll see by

---

* Not really, but *how great* would that have been, *Hamilton* fans?

the end of this chapter, some sort of productivity workflow is *essential* to ensuring that your yes is yes in our fast-paced world.

PRACTICE 2: COMMIT TO A SINGLE COMMITMENT TRACKING SYSTEM

For the sake of brevity, from here on out I will often refer to the term *Commitment Tracking System* by its acronym, CTS. I know this term might sound intimidating, but trust me, it's actually quite simple. Here's a definition:

COMMITMENT TRACKING SYSTEM: a single place to collect and track all your open loops until they are closed

Why is a *single* CTS so critical? Because open loops come flying at us from a million different directions, including (but certainly not limited to) the following:

- Our thoughts (*I'd love to write a book someday*)
- Email (*Can you email me your draft by the end of the week?*)
- Post-it Notes (*Pray for Richard's surgery*)
- Calendar (*Buy Taylor Swift tickets*)
- Slack messaging app (*We should take a company field trip there!*)
- Text messages (*Can you send me the name of your dentist again?*)
- Conversations ("*We should . . . ,*" "*Let's go to . . . ,*" "*How about we . . . ,*" "*Can you send me . . .*")

With open loops popping up in so many places, it's no wonder we feel scattered and unorganized. But here's my hunch: I don't think many people need to be sold on the idea of organizing all these commitments in a single place. Who *wouldn't* want that? What you probably need to be convinced of is why your email inbox is a terrible tool to serve as your CTS.

For most of us today, email serves as the primary source of our open loops. Thus, most people I know naturally make their email software their de facto CTS. Early in my career, I did this too. First thing in the morning, an email would come in and I'd read it to confirm there was an open loop that needed my attention. I would then mark the email as unread, star it to remind myself there was something I needed to do with the email, and then stuff it back in my inbox. As the day progressed, my emails would pile up to the point where I couldn't remember which of my twenty-three starred messages was most important or what exactly I needed to do with each one. Once I found the email I was searching for from that morning, I'd open the message again (which would now be a seventeen-email thread), hunt for the right message, and reread it to identify what I needed to do. Sound familiar?

Eventually, I realized how insane and inefficient it was to manage my stuff this way. It's really just another way of storing open loops in your brain, because each time you glance at your email, your brain has to work to remember what in the world you're supposed to *do* with all that stuff. Of course, this is a colossal waste of energy, distracting you from the work God has called you to do.

What's the solution? Extracting actionable commitments from our emails (and every other place where our open loops pop up) and discard or archive the rest. I'm going to show you exactly how to do this in practice 3, but for now I need you to commit to this: all open loops must wind up in a single CTS that *absolutely cannot be your email software.*

Okay, so what *is* the proper tool to serve as your CTS? There are two requirements for this tool:

1. It must be *portable* so you can capture open loops wherever they pop up.
2. It must be *sophisticated* enough to match the volume and complexity of your responsibilities.

Given these requirements, I am highly skeptical of any paper-based CTS. Can paper work for some people? Sure. Abraham Lincoln carried scraps of paper in his top hat to capture open loops as he walked around Washington, DC, and it clearly worked for him.[18] But I think we can all agree that our world has gotten a bit more fast paced since the 1800s. I think that once you read through the rest of the practices in this chapter, you'll be convinced that a digital tool is right for you. But the decision between a digital or physical tool isn't the most important. Again, it is the *workflow* that matters most.

My unequivocal recommendation for a tool to serve as your CTS is a piece of software called OmniFocus, but it is far from the only great tool out there. At JordanRaynor.com/RYT, I have linked to a number of tools you can use for your personal CTS. At that link, you will also find a series of free videos walking you through my personal CTS. Those videos will be immensely helpful to you as you seek to visualize how you might adopt the following practices.

PRACTICE 3: COLLECT YOUR OPEN LOOPS

At the end of the day, a Commitment Tracking System (CTS) is simply a single place to store three distinct lists:

1. Inbox List
2. Projects List
3. Actions List

The Inbox List is *not* your *email* inbox; it is a single list where everything originates in your CTS. This is the place for you to store all your open loops from your email and other inboxes until you have the time to convert those open loops into well-defined work on a Projects List and Actions List. But before I show you how to do that, it is essential that you develop the habit of getting all your open loops out of their temporary containers and onto your Inbox List in your CTS. Let's look at a couple of examples to see why and how you can quickly develop this critical habit.

You just received an email from your boss, Jill, asking you to read a lengthy memo and send back comments by the end of the week. The open loop—the thing you have a "commitment to do"—can be quickly summarized as follows: "Jill memo comments by EOW." That's what you're going to type onto the Inbox List in your CTS. If I were placing this open loop into my personal CTS, it would look like this:

Inbox List

• Jill memo comments by EOW

Now that the open loop has been extracted, *do not* mark Jill's email as unread or star or flag it to indicate there's "something" you need to do. You just decided what you need to do, so it would be terribly inefficient to force yourself to remake that decision in the future.*

Of course, email isn't the only place where open loops show up. They can pop up anywhere and anytime—while you're in the shower, talking on the phone, watching TV, and so on. Let's look at how you would capture an open loop onto the Inbox List in your CTS in one of these scenarios.

---

*If you're concerned about losing track of information in the email that you need to close the open loop, don't fret. Digital CTS tools make it easy for you to attach links to emails. If you're curious to see how this works in my personal CTS, check out the free video at JordanRaynor.com/RYT.

Recently, my wife, Kara, and I were sitting on our couch, about to watch *The West Wing* for the umpteenth time, when she said, "We really need to replace that picture above the piano now that we're a family of five." Even though this commitment isn't nearly as urgent as sending Jill comments on the memo by the end of the week, it's a commitment nonetheless. Kara has just expressed some level of commitment to doing something, and that's the definition of an open loop. If I fail to capture that open loop in my CTS, then every time I look at the wall behind the piano, my brain will subtly nag at me that there's something I need to do. So in this scenario, I pulled open the OmniFocus app on my phone and typed "Picture above the piano" onto my Inbox List.

Inbox List

- Picture above the piano

- Decide if I'm going to dinner with Jeff Morris

- Get photos into the marketing folder and share with Jenna

- Call Thom to ask about the agenda

- Sean follow-up

Notice that this open loop is not very clearly defined. Which picture? When does it need to be done? Those questions aren't important to answer yet. When putting open loops onto your Inbox List, you just need to write the minimum amount of information necessary to remind yourself of the full commitment the next time you sit down to convert those open loops into items on your Projects List and Actions List. In the next practice, I'm going to show you exactly how to do that. But first take some time to extract all your commitments from your digital inboxes, physical spaces, and mind, getting *all* your open loops onto the Inbox List in your CTS.

If you're committed to this practice and getting to "inbox zero" everywhere, go to JordanRaynor.com/RYT and watch the video on how to collect all your open loops. In that video, I will walk you through a step-by-step process for getting all your open loops onto your Inbox List the first time.

PRACTICE 4: DEFINE YOUR WORK

If you went through the entire process of collecting all your open loops onto the Inbox List in your Commitment Tracking System (CTS), you're likely feeling some combination of three things: relief, overwhelm, and guilt. Relief that maybe for the first time ever you have collected all your commitments in a single place, overwhelm because you can now see clearly how much you have to do, and guilt over open loops that remind you of where you've dropped the ball. When I first went through this process, I experienced all three of those emotions. Before we go any further, I want you to take a breath and hear two words of encouragement.

First, if you're overwhelmed, remember this truth from chapter 1: *God doesn't need you to finish your to-do list.* You will *never* complete everything you just put into your CTS, and that's okay.

Second, if you have open loops that represent commitments you've broken with yourself and others, remember the gospel and *extend yourself grace.* God showed you grace when you were his enemy (see Romans 5:10). Surely you can give yourself grace for forgetting to call your grandmother on her birthday.

God showed you grace when you were his enemy. Surely you can give yourself grace for forgetting to call your grandmother.

Even with that encouragement, you may still feel overwhelmed and stressed. Why? Because although you have finally captured all your open loops, your brain is still trying to decide *precisely* what needs to be done about each of them. Remember the participants in Dr. Baumeister's study: the students who were most able to focus on the task at hand were the ones who made "a *plan*" for what they needed to do in the future. It's not enough to place open loops on the Inbox List of your CTS. To get open loops fully off of your brain, you must make a plan for how you will close them in the future. That's what you're going to learn to do in this practice as you transition items from your Inbox List to the Projects List and Actions List in your CTS. This is the step in which you finally define your work.

Now, you're probably thinking, *Define my work? I think my work is pretty clearly defined, Jordan.* Trust me, it's not. Before we roll up our sleeves again, let me explain.

Most of our great-grandparents didn't have to define their work. Mine grew up rolling cigars in Tampa, Florida, where their work was clear-cut: take the tobacco leaf, roll the tobacco leaf, slap on a label, rinse and repeat. Most of us aren't doing this type of factory work today (as important and God-honoring as this work is).* Economists would describe most of us as "knowledge workers," and the essence of knowledge work is that you have to think and define what the work is before you sit down to do it. As Stephen Covey said, "All things

---

*One of my favorite episodes of my podcast was with Dave Hataj, the owner of a gear factory, talking about the God-given dignity of blue-collar work. You'll find the link to the episode at JordanRaynor.com/RYT.

are created twice. There's a mental or first creation, and a physical or second creation, to all things."[19]

This partially explains why so many items on our to-do lists have been there for so long. Our to-do lists are filled with open loops that have not been clearly defined as something we can actually *do* and *act upon*. We have yet to do the mental "first creation" of defining our work as tangible things we can do for the glory of God and the good of others.

Many people's to-do lists are filled with items such as "Doctor's appointment," "Halloween," and "Airbnb for vacation." Looking at a list like this will bring more stress than calm because although those items represent a valuable reminder of an open loop, your brain is still begging you to make decisions about what precisely these open loops are and how you're going to close them.

This is why your Inbox List is not enough. To ensure your yes is yes and that you are maximally productive, you have to convert the open loops on your Inbox List into well-defined work on your Projects List and Actions List. How? By answering the following five questions.

Question #1: Am I Still Committed to Closing This Open Loop?

If you have an overwhelming number of items on your Inbox List, consider asking the more rigorous version of this question: "Would anything happen if I *never* completed this?"

If the answer to any variation of this question is no, delete the open loop from your Inbox List and move on to the next item. (In case you're curious, I delete roughly a quarter of my open loops with this first question.) If the answer is yes, move on to the next question.

Question #2: What Is My Actual Desired Outcome?

Take a second to clarify what your true desired outcome is with your open loop. In other words, what needs to happen for your brain to close the loop on this item forever?

Let's go back to the example I shared before about replacing the family picture above our piano. In that example, I wrote down the open loop as "Picture above piano" on the Inbox List in my CTS. But that desired outcome isn't concrete enough. I must do the mental "first creation" of defining more clearly what exactly this means to me and what needs to happen for me to close this open loop and call it "done." So, on my Inbox List, I will replace the text "Picture above piano" with a more clearly defined outcome, such as "Replace the family picture above the piano," and move on to the next question in our workflow.

Inbox List

- ~~Picture above the piano~~

- Replace the family picture above the piano

- Decide if I'm going to dinner with Jeff Morris

- Get photos into the marketing folder and share with Jenna

- Call Thom to ask about the agenda

- Sean follow-up

Question #3: Will It Take More Than One Action to Close This Open Loop?

This question is *critical*. Let's look at another example to see why.

Let's say I have an item on my Inbox List that reads, "Send Jen a copy of *Redeeming Your Time*." On the surface, it might look like it will take only one action to close this open loop, but in reality, there are quite a number of actions I need to take to achieve this desired outcome. I need to search for Jen's address. When I realize I don't have her address, I need to email her to ask for it. Then I need to wait for Jen's reply. Finally, once Jen sends me her address, I need to order the book and ship it to her home.

In this workflow, these types of open loops that require more than one action to complete are called "projects." Of course, that definition encompasses *many* things that you would have never historically referred to as projects. But the distinction between the Projects List and Actions List in your CTS could not be more important in ensuring your yes is yes. Here's why: a project serves as a "stake in the ground" reminding you that even though you may have completed some action associated with a desired outcome, you still have an open loop, as the ultimate desired outcome has yet to be achieved.[20] Let me offer one more example to make this clearer.

After I'm done recording an episode of my podcast, I send the audio files to my producer, Chris. Chris then decides which edits to make and sends those requested edits to a technical editor to produce the final episode. The technical editor makes edits and sends the final audio file to Chris, who then uploads the episode as a draft in our podcast-hosting software. I then review the draft and schedule the episode to be published.

I can't close my open loop until we accomplish the desired outcome: "Publish episode 76 of the podcast before January 6." If I had only "Record episode 76 of the podcast" or "Send the files to Chris" written down, I would have checked those individual actions off and could have easily forgotten about the bigger desired outcome until it was too late and I got a bunch of hysterical emails from you all begging for the next episode (one can dream, right?).

Like you, I have a lot going on. I can't afford to have my brain working overtime to remember deadlines, desired outcomes, and what my team and I are expected to do next. To operate at my highest potential, I have to track those open loops outside my head and in my CTS until they are fully closed. As David Allen explained, "The list of projects is the compilation of finish lines we put before us to keep our next actions moving on all tracks appropriately."[21]

As you go through this workflow, you'll see that *most* of your desired outcomes are projects. So, look at one of the items on your Inbox List. Will it take more than one action to close this loop and achieve your desired outcome?

If yes, cut your desired outcome from your Inbox List, paste it onto the Projects List in your CTS, and move on to question 4 to define the next action for your project.*

Projects List

- Replace the family picture above the piano

- Publish episode 76 of the podcast before January 6
  (due January 6, 2022)

- Deliver a revised manuscript to Becky
  (due January 25, 2022)

---

*Got an overwhelming number of projects in your CTS? See how I organize my projects into folders in the video at JordanRaynor.com/RYT.

If it will *not* take more than one action to close your open loop, then you've already identified the next action you need to take. Thus, you can skip question 4 and move on to the fifth and final question in this workflow.

Question #4: What's the Next Action?

More concretely, what is the next *physical* thing you can envision yourself doing to move one step closer to completing your project? In the words of (spoiler alert!) Queen Anna of Arendelle, a next action is "the next right thing"²² you can do to make progress toward closing your open loop.

Why is it not enough to have a list of projects? Why must you define next actions for each item on your Projects List? Because you can't actually *do* a project; you can only do physical actions that move a project forward.

Many people feel overwhelmed with their to-do lists because there's nothing they can physically *do* on their lists. Go back to the list I mentioned before:

- Doctor's appointment
- Halloween
- Airbnb for vacation

Those aren't to-dos. You can't *do* Halloween. These are all open loops that need to be clearly defined and converted into projects (which you did in question 3) *and* physical actions you can take to bring those projects closer to completion. If you fail to define physical next actions for each project, you will waste precious brainpower every time you look at your Projects List and try to remember exactly what needs to happen to bring those initiatives one step closer to being done.

Many people feel overwhelmed with their to-do lists because there's nothing they can physically do on their lists.

A few years ago, I lost fifty pounds in just a few months. When people would ask me how I did it, I think I frustrated them with the simplicity of my answer: I converted an amorphous open loop on my Inbox List ("lose weight") into a well-defined item on my Projects List ("Lose fifty pounds by December 31") and finally defined the next *physical action* I could take toward that end ("Download MyFitness-Pal to track my calories"). Then I defined the next action after that (a recurring to-do to "Log calories for what I ate today in MFP"). And so on and so on.

And that was it. Truly. Sounds simple? It is. And *anyone* can do it, including you. Dr. Martin Luther King Jr. once said, "You don't have to see the whole staircase, just take the first step."[23] That's what defining the next action for each of your projects is all about and why this question is so important.

As you've likely guessed by now, the next action for each item on your Projects List will live on the Actions List in your CTS. But before you add items to that third and final list, there's one more question you need to ask.

Question #5: Will It Take Less Than Two Minutes to Complete This Action?

If yes, do it right now. Why? Because it's more efficient to complete the task than it is to store it in your Commitment Tracking System (CTS) and do it later.

If you take only one thing from this chapter, this "two-minute rule" alone could change your life. This has been a game changer for me and pretty much anyone I've ever taught this workflow to.

If the action will take longer than two minutes to complete, add it to the Actions List in your CTS. Although your Projects List serves as a comprehensive inventory of all the finish lines of your commitments, your Actions List serves as your functional to-do list, enabling you to make progress toward those finish lines each day.*

Actions List

- Scroll through Photos app on phone to find our best family picture

- Read through Becky's comments on chapter 2 of *Redeeming Your Time*

- Read The Ringer's profile on Taylor Swift

If there is a deadline associated with an item on your Actions List or Projects List, add that date to the item in your CTS. *But be sure to keep those deadlines sacred.* Don't assign dates to things you *want* to get done on a specific date. Assign deadlines only for things that absolutely *must* get done at a specific time. Why? Because when your day blows up with an unexpected meeting or you need to go pick up your kid who's throwing up at school, you must be able to quickly identify

---

*If you're wondering why projects and actions don't live on the same list, check out the free videos that correspond to this chapter at JordanRaynor.com/RYT. As you'll see, digital CTS tools like the one I use make it easy to view your Projects List and Actions List separately or together.

what's *actually* due today so you can renegotiate your commitments accordingly.

Why not keep those deadlined items on your calendar? Because as your responsibilities grow (and as you do the work in this book and earn the trust of those around you, they *will* grow), your calendar will quickly become overwhelmed. You need to keep your calendar clear to focus only on appointments you have made with others and yourself (more on this in chapters 5 and 7).

One more thing before we wrap up this workflow. Oftentimes, the next action on a project is something you're waiting on from somebody else. For example, after I record an episode of my podcast, the next action for my project ("Publish Episode 76 of the podcast before January 6") is to "Wait for Chris to notify me that Episode 76 is ready for my review." Treat these actions just as you would treat one that you're personally responsible for: track it on your Actions List.

Actions List

- Wait for Chris to notify me that episode 76 is ready for my review
  (due January 4, 2022)

- Scroll through Photos app on phone to find our best family picture

- Read through Becky's comments on chapter 2 of *Redeeming Your Time*

- Read The Ringer's profile on Taylor Swift

Okay, now that we've made it through the five questions for defining your work, look at page 49 for a flowchart that maps out how everything fits together. If you'd like, you can download a copy of this for free at JordanRaynor.com/RYT.

You might be thinking, *It's going to take the whole day to work through these questions for everything in my CTS!* Trust me, it's not. With just a little bit of practice, you'll be able to answer all five questions in less than thirty seconds for most items on your Inbox List. Don't believe me? Watch me process some items in my personal CTS at JordanRaynor.com/RYT.

Okay, Jordan, maybe I can learn to do this, but come on, a flowchart *for figuring out how to hang a picture? This all seems a bit much.*

Let me close out this practice by explaining why it's not. Here's the deal: all five of these questions are ones you are *already* asking yourself every time you get something done. Of course, you probably aren't consciously asking them, and you likely aren't using this exact terminology, but I promise, you are asking them. This workflow simply batches the work of defining your work. If, for example, you suspect your mobile phone is on its last leg and you'll soon need a new one, you will have to define the next action for that project eventually. The problem is that most people wait until their phone dies in the middle of an important call, ensuring the next action is "Drive as quickly as possible to the Apple Store." You have a choice: you can define your work either "when it shows up, or when it blows up."[24] Which will you choose?

PRACTICE 5: MAINTAIN YOUR COMMITMENT TRACKING SYSTEM

If you've completed practices 1 through 4, the hard part is over. The heavy lifting is done! You are well on your way to redeeming your time, and you probably feel as though you're on top of the world.

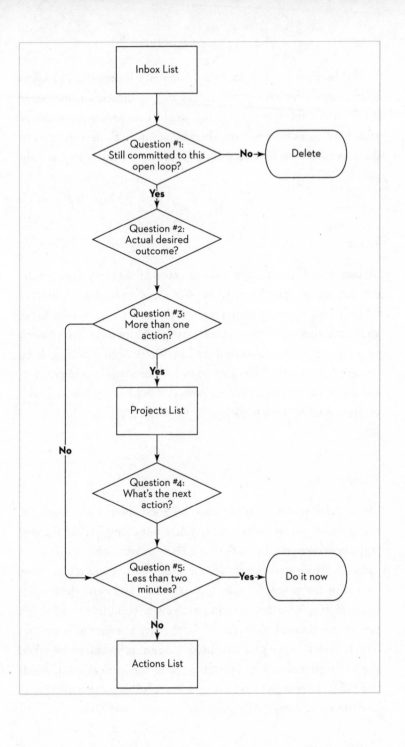

But here's the sad truth: this is where most people fail. I know many people who have spent hours setting up their CTS, only to see it fall apart a few weeks later. *That doesn't have to be you.* To ensure your hard work isn't in vain, there's one more thing you need to do: you must commit to a daily and weekly workflow to maintain your CTS.

Daily

To keep your CTS in shape, you must spend time every single workday extracting open loops from your email and other temporary inboxes, placing those open loops on the Inbox List in your CTS, and converting each item on your Inbox List into well-defined work on your Projects List and Actions List. That's right: I'm suggesting you get to "inbox zero" every single day. As the workflows in practices 3 and 4 become habit, this entire process should take you only fifteen to thirty minutes each workday.

Weekly

David Allen wrote, "You can only feel good about what you're not doing when you *know* everything you're not doing."[25] And the way you can assure your brain that you know what you're not doing is by committing to a weekly review. This is when you review your "stakes in the ground"—your Projects List—and close those open loops forever by either marking projects as complete or adding a new next action to your Actions List to move a project forward. The weekly review is the glue that holds this entire workflow together. For a more detailed, step-by-step guide to this critical habit, watch the video I recorded on how to have a killer weekly review at JordanRaynor.com/RYT.

COLLECTING THE PUZZLE PIECES

Now that we've collected our commitments in a single place, how do we prioritize our projects and actions to ensure we are focusing on the work that matters most? We must first create space to think and explore what in our CTS truly matters by dissenting from the kingdom of noise. That's the piece of the puzzle we will collect in chapter 3.

CHAPTER 3

DISSENT FROM THE KINGDOM OF NOISE

To redeem our time in the model of our Redeemer, we must fight to block out noise and create room for silence, stillness, and reflection.

I t's one of the most iconic photographs in American history: Dr. Martin Luther King Jr. is dressed in a suit and tie, looking out on a massive sea of people beneath him. The crowd of more than 250,000 people is erupting in applause for King and the speech he just delivered about his dream for America.[1] King smiles and waves back at the crowd as they line the reflecting pool, which stands between King's podium at the Lincoln Memorial and the Washington Monument. Years after the photograph is snapped, history remembers this moment as the most productive of King's life. But it may never have happened had King not cultivated his own private "reflecting pools" in the midst of the noisy 1950s and '60s.

Nine years before delivering his historic speech, King began pastoring a church in Montgomery, Alabama—the city that would become ground zero for the civil rights movement when Rosa Parks was arrested for refusing to give up her seat for a white passenger and move to the back of a bus. In peaceful protest of this injustice, Montgomery's black residents staged a yearlong boycott of the bus system, which catapulted King into the national spotlight.

From that moment on, life in Montgomery was chaotic and noisy for King. As he explained in his autobiography, "From early morning to late at night my telephone rang and my doorbell was seldom silent."[2] Everyone wanted a piece of King, making it impossible for him to be still and reflect on which of his competing priorities were most important to moving civil rights forward. "I felt terribly frustrated over my inability to retreat, concentrate, and reflect," he wrote.[3]

So strong was King's conviction of the need for quiet reflection that he decided to make a dramatic change: he moved his family from Montgomery to Atlanta, Georgia, where he would have the silence he needed "to meditate and think through the total struggle ahead. . . . I knew that I could not continue to live with such a tension-filled schedule. . . . My failure to reflect would do harm not only to me as a person, but to the total movement. For that reason I felt a moral obligation to do it."[4]

Like King, you and I have a moral obligation to seek out solitude as we try to redeem our time. Why? Because now more than ever, we are living in what C. S. Lewis's devil Screwtape called "the Kingdom of Noise."[5]

You and I have a moral obligation to seek out solitude as we try to redeem our time.

THE KINGDOM OF NOISE

We live in a time of an unprecedented amount of noise. And I'm not referring to just the obvious increase in *external* noise created by nonstop news and entertainment and the buzzing of the devices in our pockets and purses; I'm primarily referring to what all that external noise creates—namely, *internal* noise. For the sake of clarity, allow me to offer my own definition of *noise* to guide the rest of this chapter.

NOISE: external information and entertainment that block our ability to be silent and reflective

Today, we have almost completely eradicated the silence and reflection Dr. King fought so hard to protect. As we'll see in a minute, those are *critical* ingredients for redeeming our time.

But before I try to convince you that noise is connected to our perpetual time-management problems, I need to first share a bit of my personal journey down this road, because if you knew me ten years ago, you wouldn't recognize the person speaking to you in this chapter.

I was addicted to noise from an early age. Even before smartphones (I know, dating myself), I was always consuming entertainment and information, *especially* the news. One of my most embarrassing childhood pastimes was cutting out pictures of my favorite politicians from the newspaper and turning them into collages. Yes, hanging there in my bedroom were photomontages of George W. Bush, Condoleezza Rice, Cory Booker, and, of course, my teenage crush Barbara Bush.* Embarassing, I know.

In college, my love of noise reached a new level with the advent of smartphones. I was one of the few students who brought a Black-Berry to campus in 2004. I did this not because it was cool (trust me, it wasn't) but because I couldn't bear missing a piece of breaking news or, heaven forbid, five minutes of boredom. Once social media came along, it was game over as my phone was practically glued to my hands. I was constantly liking, texting, and tweeting. I was Tom Haverford from *Parks and Recreation,* only worse.†

Why go through this embarrassing, self-deprecating exercise and risk having you write me off as a crazy person? So that I can contrast the old Jordan from a decade ago with the new Jordan today.

Whereas old Jordan would tweet a dozen times each day, today I now personally tweet about a dozen times each year. Whereas old

---

*W.'s daughter, not H. W.'s wife.

†Don't believe me? Check out this cringeworthy tweet I posted on August 25, 2009: "I prescheduled this tweet just so I could say I technically tweeted while in the juror box." Seriously, I was "the *woooorst.*"

Jordan would easily spend four to five hours on his smartphone each day, this week I'm averaging thirty-three minutes of daily screen time. Whereas old Jordan lived and died with each breaking news alert, today I consume virtually zero news. No news websites. No newspapers. No podcasts. Nothing. I have almost entirely dissented from the kingdom of noise. If my twenty-four-year-old self lived life at volume ten, thirty-four-year-old Jordan lives life at volume two.

Now, before you skip this chapter and dismiss me as a curmudgeon, let me assure you that I *don't* live at volume zero. I am not a recluse and have no plans to be. And unlike some time-management books, I am not going to tell you that you need to delete Instagram or get rid of your smartphone to redeem your time. I still own, use, and *love* my iPhone. I love having Maps, Timehop, YouVersion's Bible app, and OmniFocus in my pocket. I love that I can watch Netflix on my phone if I'm stuck in an airport. And I love that I can listen to *Hamilton* and Taylor Swift from the back of a car that I hailed from an app on my phone.

These are *good* things, all made possible by the noisiest device I own. But over the years, God has graciously shown me that although my phone and the other noisy devices in my life can be vehicles for good, they also have *incredible* power to drown out all semblance of silence, solitude, and reflection.

Hang on a second, Jordan. What in the world does noise and the pursuit of silence have to do with time management and productivity? At least five things.

FIVE WAYS NOISE LIMITS OUR ABILITY TO REDEEM TIME

#1: Noise Limits Our Ability to Think

Pastor Kevin DeYoung once wrote, "We are always engaged with our thumbs, but rarely engaged with our thoughts."[6] That's spot-on.

When our minds are filled with noise, there is simply no mental space to think. And if we can't think clearly, we can't prioritize our to-do lists and effectively engage with the work God has given us to do. Good work requires good thought, and good thought requires great solitude. But you can't be alone with your own thoughts until you stop voluntarily drowning in information and other people's opinions. Bestselling author Ryan Holiday said it well:

> It's very difficult to think or act clearly (to say nothing of being happy) when we are drowning in information. It's why lawyers attempt to bury the other side in paper. It's why intelligence operatives flood the enemy with propaganda, so they'll lose the scent of the truth. It's not a coincidence that the goal of these tactics is casually referred to as analysis *paralysis*.[7]

Shortly after CNN introduced the novel idea of twenty-four-hour news in the 1980s, political scientists began studying the effects that nonstop news had on the ability for politicians to make decisions. Unsurprisingly, they found that in "the absence of quiet time"[8] away from the media frenzy, elected officials' "decisions are made in haste, sometimes dangerously so."[9]

Scientists call this phenomenon the CNN effect, and although it may have primarily affected presidents and prime ministers in the 1980s and '90s, it affects nearly everyone today. We are drowning in a relentless flood of information—not just from CNN and other news services, but from podcasts, blogs, and social media. And, of course, these sources of noise don't create just *information* overload but *opinion* overload too.

When I was CEO of the tech start-up Threshold 360, one of our investors asked me, "What's the number one skill we should be looking for as we consider investing in other founders and CEOs?" My answer came easily: "The ability to discern the essential from the noise."

In a start-up—really, in *any* work today—new information and opinions come flying at you from every direction. Every time you open your email or social media feed, you see new market research, various product ideas, and messages from four different people who believe that attending *their* meetings is the best use of your time. This, of course, makes it extremely hard to discern and focus on what matters. As one Nobel Prize winner said, "A wealth of information creates a poverty of attention."[10]

But information in and of itself isn't bad. Information is a gift! The problem is when the information flow *never stops*. To discern the essential from the noise, at some point you have to turn off the information-and-opinion fire hose, get quiet, and simply *think*. Only in solitude can you separate the important from the unimportant and avoid getting stuck in the "thick of thin things."[11] Mister Rogers said it best: "Just be quiet and think. It'll make all the difference in the world."[12]

Noise limits our ability to think. And if we don't have space to think, we can't discern the essential from the noise and prioritize our to-do lists. And if we can't prioritize, we can't focus on the work we believe God has called us to do.

#2: Noise Limits Our Ability to Be Creative

My favorite TV show wouldn't exist if it weren't for boredom. That's what led Aaron Sorkin to first try his hand at writing dialogue, which led to his career writing hits such as *The West Wing* (the all-time favorite of yours truly), *The Social Network,* and *Moneyball.* Sorkin explained how it happened:

There was this one night, I was living in . . . a tiny studio apartment . . . and everyone I knew was out of town. I didn't have three dollars in my pocket. And in this apartment was a semi-automatic typewriter. . . . The TV was broken. The stereo was broken. The only thing to do was to put a piece of paper in that typewriter and start typing. . . . [It was] pure boredom. . . . And I stayed up all night writing, and I feel like that night has never ended.[13]

Like Sorkin, C. S. Lewis may never have written the Chronicles of Narnia had it not been for boredom. Lewis grew up in the early 1900s in the Irish countryside, where there wasn't much to do, especially on the Emerald Isle's frequent rainy days. As his biographer pointed out, Lewis and his brother "spent many hours making up their own stories. . . . I suppose the beginnings of Narnia can be seen in this childhood occupation, which was their way of combating the boredom of hours spent in the house while the soft Irish rain fell slowly and steadily outside."[14]

Of course, boredom—which we could define as a lack of noise—is much rarer today than it was for Sorkin in the 1980s or Lewis in the early 1900s. With all the noise in our lives today, we've made boredom nearly extinct, and that's a problem because a lack of noise is essential to creativity.

Let's make this personal: Where do *you* have *your* most creative ideas? If this were a question on *Family Feud*, I can almost guarantee the top answer would be "In the shower." Why? Because the shower is one of the last places on earth that isn't filled with noise. It's one of the only places we can find solitude.

Noise limits our opportunities to be bored and thus creative. And if we don't have the space to work out our God-given gift of creativity, it will be far more difficult to be productive.

#3: Noise Limits Our Ability to Cultivate Depth

In chapter 5, we will explore in detail the critical habit of doing undistracted "deep work." For now, all you need to know is that dissenting from the kingdom of noise is a prerequisite for doing high-quality, focused work. The research shows that if you spend all your time away from your desk filling your mind with noise, you will have a much harder time focusing on your work when you want to. To go deep when you're ready, you have to "wean your mind from a dependence on distraction."[15]

Of course, our lack of silence and reflection doesn't limit our ability to cultivate depth just at work but is equally harmful for engaging deeply at home. God didn't design our minds to merely receive information. He created us to think about and make creative connections between various inputs. So what happens when we fail to make the time to do this thinking alone? We do it when we're with others: our spouses, kids, and friends. Even if the *external* noise is turned down (phones are out of sight, the TV is off, and so on), the *internal* noise is still blaring because your brain is trying to process and connect the information you received throughout the day.

> *God didn't design our minds to merely receive information. He created us to think about and make creative connections between various inputs.*

When I fail to adopt the practices I'm going to share in this chapter, it's a major problem for me. If I've had a day with no silence and time to think, I'll be sitting at the dinner table, physically present with my wife and kids but totally absent mentally. One of my daughters will ask me a question and I'll miss it because I'm trying to do the thinking my brain *has* to do to sort through all the information I consumed during the day.

Instead of focusing on my wife and kids, I'm thinking, *How does that project connect with this one? Couldn't that new hire help me kill two birds with one stone?* My lack of silence and solitude has blocked my ability to be fully present in the moment. That's what nonstop noise does: it limits our ability to cultivate depth at work and at home, thwarting our attempts to be purposeful, present, and productive.

#4: Noise Limits Our Ability to Be at Peace

Three things happened in 2007. First, Steve Jobs introduced the iPhone, ushering in a future in which the lack of a smartphone is almost unheard of in the developed world. Second, Americans started a ten-year 59 percent decrease in productivity compared to the previous decade.[16] And third, seemingly out of nowhere, anxiety and other mental health issues exploded around the globe, especially in teenagers. The timing of these three events is not a coincidence. The rising volume of the kingdom of noise is making us less productive and significantly more anxious.

Dr. Jean Twenge, a professor at San Diego State University, has been studying psychological trends in young people for more than twenty-five years. Around 2012, Twenge noticed a dramatic shift in the mental health patterns of kids born between 1995 and 2012, a generation she calls iGen. Among this generation, "rates of teen depression and suicide have skyrocketed," Twenge wrote.[17] Looking at the data, she said,

> The gentle slopes of the line graphs became steep mountains and sheer cliffs, and many of the distinctive characteristics of the Millennial generation [which preceded iGen] began to disappear. In all my analyses of generational data—some reaching back to the 1930s—I had never seen anything like it. . . .
>
> It's not an exaggeration to describe iGen as being on the brink of the worst mental-health crisis in decades.[18]

Dr. Twenge added that these spikes in anxiety corresponded to "exactly the moment when the proportion of Americans who owned a smartphone surpassed 50 percent."[19]

The data is becoming clearer and clearer: smartphones—the devices responsible for much, if not most, of the noise in our lives today—are robbing us of silence and making us more anxious at work and home.

Of course, it's not just smartphones that lead to anxiety and a lack of peace—it's noise in general. One of the other chief culprits in this problem is our culture of nonstop news. According to *Time* magazine,

> More than half of Americans say the news causes them stress, and many report feeling anxiety, fatigue or sleep loss as a result. . . . Yet one in 10 adults checks the news every hour, and fully 20% of Americans report "constantly" monitoring their social media feeds—which often exposes them to the latest news headlines, whether they like it or not.[20]

This is certifiably *insane*. We are literally *making ourselves* anxious by welcoming all this noise into our lives.

I'm not immune to this problem. As I mentioned previously, I consume virtually no news. But when my friends notify me of a major event that directly affects my life and work, I'll pull open a news website to get the information I need. That's exactly what happened during the COVID-19 pandemic.

When I heard about the virus from a few friends, I started checking news websites for information about school closures, social-distancing directives, and mask mandates. Obviously, this information was highly relevant to me. But in the search for that important information, I quickly stumbled into the quicksand that is most digital news services, scanning headlines from the ridiculous ("Hulk Hogan: 'Maybe We Don't Need a Vaccine'")[21] to the fear inducing ("750,000 People in North Carolina Could Be Infected by June").[22] While Hulk Hogan's antics were mildly entertaining and North Carolinians were now in my prayers, the fact was that this news didn't affect me *at all*.

A couple of days after my rare entrance back into the kingdom of noise, I was experiencing a level of anxiety I had *never* felt before. That's when I read Philippians 4:6–8:

Do not be anxious about anything, but in every situation, by prayer and petition, with thanksgiving, present your requests to God. And the peace of God, which transcends all understanding, will guard your hearts and your minds in Christ Jesus.

Finally, brothers and sisters, whatever is true, whatever is noble, whatever is right, whatever is pure, whatever is lovely, whatever is admirable—if anything is excellent or praiseworthy—think about such things.

Up until reading this passage during the COVID-19 pandemic, I had never connected verses 6 and 8 before. But of course, there they are, back to back, separated only by verse 7. I think Paul is telling us that part of the solution to our anxiety is found in what we're choosing to think about—the noise and information we are inviting into our minds. Most news is *not* true, noble, right, pure, lovely, or admirable. *It's just noise.* And much like our smartphones, news creates anxiety in our lives, making it harder for us to focus on the work God has given us to do.

#5: Noise Limits Our Ability to Listen to God's Voice

This final way that noise influences our ability to redeem our time is the most important. Pastor John Mark Comer said it best: "The noise of the modern world makes us deaf to the voice of God, drowning out the one input we most need."[23] By filling our lives with noise, we are becoming the "wicked man" of Psalm 10:4, who "in all his thoughts" has "no room for God." We are inflicting ourselves with what Timothy Keller called "the torture of divine absence."[24]

Make no mistake: noise is an intentional part of the Enemy's plan to keep us from redeeming our time. C. S. Lewis articulated this well in *The Screwtape Letters* when his fictional senior demon says to his protégé, "Music and silence—how I detest them both! . . . We will make the whole universe a noise in the end. . . . The melodies and silences of Heaven will be shouted down in the end."[25]

But the problem is less about what noise we allow *into* our minds and more about what noise we're keeping *out*—namely, our own thoughts and ability to listen to God's voice.

I think it's important to note here the difference between *hearing* the voice of God and *listening* to it. We *hear* his voice when we read his Word. But here's the thing: "quiet times" aren't actually that quiet. We read. We study. We are quiet in the sense that we aren't speaking, but our minds are still noisy because we are still consuming information. When we read and study God's Word, we *hear* his voice, but it takes silence and reflection to *listen* to his voice and connect his Word to our lives.

In Psalm 46:10, our Father invites us to "be still, and know that [he is] God." Commenting on this verse, Emily P. Freeman said,

> There's a reason why God invites us to be still first: the stillness makes way for the knowing. . . . Stillness is to my soul as decluttering is to my home. Silence and stillness are how I sift through the day's input. The silence serves as a colander, helping me discern what I need to hold on to and allowing what I don't need to fall gently away, making space to access courage and creativity, quieting to hear the voice of God.[26]

That's it. Silence, stillness, solitude, reflection—*that's* the difference between hearing God's Word and listening to his voice.

Silence, stillness, solitude, reflection—that's the difference between hearing God's Word and listening to his voice.

If you listen to my podcast, you know that I end every conversation by asking my guest for a single piece of advice to leave listeners with as we seek to redeem our time for the glory of God and the good of others. I once had the honor of posing that question to my all-time favorite writer, Timothy Keller, and I was a bit surprised by his answer. He said, "When you get to the end of your life, you are going to say, 'I should have put way more time into prayer, reading, and *solitude*'" (emphasis added).[27] I expected him to say prayer. I expected him to say reading the Word. But *solitude*? I was shocked that made the list.

Another one of my favorite writers and pastors, John Mark Comer, assigned equal weight to our need for silence. In his terrific book *The Ruthless Elimination of Hurry,* Comer offered "four practices for unhurrying your life."[28] The "most important," according to Comer? "Silence and solitude."[29]

Why do these wise pastors assign so much importance to dissenting from the kingdom of noise? Because they know that Jesus himself assigned so much importance to silence during his time on earth.

JESUS'S LONELY PLACES

The number of times the Gospels mention Jesus withdrawing to a solitary place is staggering. In the third gospel alone, Luke mentions Jesus's love of lonely places *three times* in just one and a half chapters (see 4:42; 5:16; 6:12).

My favorite example of Jesus's pursuit of solitude is when "he withdrew by boat privately to a solitary place" to get away from the crowds (Matthew 14:13). So important was silence to Jesus that he would literally just jump into a boat to get away from all the noise to pray, think, and *listen* to his Father's voice.

And oh by the way, the busier Jesus got, the *more* he sought out silence. Luke 5:15–16 says that as "the news about him spread all the more . . . Jesus often withdrew to lonely places and prayed."

Given our comparative lack of silent solitude today, it can be easy to read these verses and feel sorry that Jesus spent so much time in lonely spaces. *Poor Jesus,* we think. *Can't the disciples step up and give their friend some company?* But as I hope you're beginning to see, lonely places aren't places of weakness. They are places of great strength.

Nowhere is this more vivid than the first time the Gospels show Jesus alone. Immediately after being baptized by John the Baptist, "Jesus was led by the Spirit into the wilderness to be tempted by the devil" (Matthew 4:1). It was there that Jesus spent forty days hungry and alone. On the surface, it appears that this lonely place was a place of weakness. But Luke 4:14 tells us that Jesus returned from the wilderness *"in the power of the Spirit."* It was only after spending forty days in quiet solitude that Jesus was ready to do the work of his Father. As John Mark Comer points out, "That's why, over and over again, you see Jesus come back to [lonely places]."[30]

As we'll see throughout this book, Jesus was *crazy* intentional and focused about how he spent his time on earth. As we apprentice ourselves to him and seek to model his habits as we redeem our time for his purposes, we simply can't ignore the phenomenal amount of time Jesus spent dissenting from the kingdom of noise, which brings us to the third principle of this book:

PRINCIPLE #3
DISSENT FROM THE KINGDOM OF NOISE

To redeem our time in the model of our Redeemer, we must fight to block out noise and create room for silence, stillness, and reflection.

Before we examine what it looks like to practice this principle in our modern age, we have to answer this question: Why is silence so rare? Of course, we've already seen the most obvious answer to that question: the "attention economy conglomerates"[31] (smartphone manufacturers, news outlets, social media services, and so on) are powerful and sophisticated forces that profit from our lack of silence. But they are not the only ones to blame. We have to take some responsibility for our lack of silence because, if we're honest, most of us are afraid of what we'll hear if the noise ever stops.

There's an old word called *acedia* that describes what I'm talking about. Pastor Richard John Neuhaus defined it this way: "Acedia is evenings without number obliterated by television, evenings neither of entertainment nor of education but of narcoticized defense against time and duty. Above all, acedia is apathy, the refusal to engage the pathos of other lives and of God's life with them."[32]

"Narcoticized defense against time and duty." Man, that one stings. Is *that* what we're up to when we refuse to listen to silence? Pastor Kevin DeYoung said it is:

> For too many of us, the hustle and bustle of electronic activity is a sad expression of a deeper acedia. . . . We want to be harried and hassled and busy. Unconsciously, we want the very things we complain about. For if we had leisure [or silence], we would look at ourselves and listen to our hearts and see the great gaping hole in our hearts and be terrified, because that hole is so big that nothing but God can fill it.[33]

Believer, you have no need to fear silence. Why? Because the gospel of Jesus Christ has the power to fill the God-shaped hole inside your heart. Social media likes will never cover it. Your phone can't paper over it. Nonstop information and entertainment will never fill it. Only Jesus can, *and he has.* But he didn't fill that hole so we could sit around and pass the time consuming until eternity; he filled the hole to make us whole, freeing us to create a world that's closer to his kingdom. Jesus has filled our hearts so that we would "fill the earth" (Genesis 1:28) with his glory by doing good works for others.

But we can't do that work if our lives are filled with noise and acedia. In the words of Picasso, "Without great solitude no serious work is possible."[34] With that in mind, let's get to work dissenting from the kingdom of noise.

The first five practices in this chapter will help you turn down the noise in your life, while the final four will help you cultivate thinking, creativity, and opportunities to listen to God's voice once the noise has been drowned out.

PRACTICE 1: LET YOUR FRIENDS CURATE INFORMATION FOR YOU

Let's be honest: we *love* being the first to know something. We love being the first to share a rumor at work, being the one who discovers a great new book or musician, or being the first to text breaking news to our friends. In the words of Ryan Holiday, "There is ego in trying to stay up on everything . . . in trying to appear the most informed person in the room."[35]

But it's not just ego that's embedded in our desire to be in the know—it's also subtle idolatry. Jen Wilkin nailed it: "Our insatiable desire for information is a clear sign that we covet the divine omniscience. . . . We must observe God's good boundaries for how much information we can process."[36]

God has not designed our brains to process unlimited information. That's why I recommend practicing what bestselling author Tim Ferriss called "selective ignorance."[37] Ralph Waldo Emerson once said, "There are many things of which a wise man might wish to be ignorant."[38] That pretty much sums up my approach to news, social media, and other information services. Unless there's a specific piece of information I'm looking for, I stay off these services entirely.

But here's the thing: believe it or not, I'm *not* totally ignorant. Want to know my secret? If you eliminate or significantly reduce your time spent consuming information, your friends will curate information *for you.*

If you eliminate or significantly reduce your time spent consuming information, your friends will curate information for you.

I hear about everything that truly matters to my life and work. When Timothy Keller tweeted that he had been diagnosed with pancreatic cancer, *eight* of my friends texted me within minutes of the news breaking. I hear about pandemics, hurricanes, race riots, media trends, and rumors about every new Taylor Swift album. And I hear about all these things without having to spend a single moment wading through the 99.9 percent of content on social media and news websites that is anxiety inducing or totally meaningless to me. My friends curate all this *for me*. In a way, this is a bizarre form of delegation. Of course, my friends don't know that I've delegated this work to them, but that's precisely what I've done.*

This practice isn't selfish. My friends choose to consume more information than I do. By all means, *please* try to convince your friends to join you in a "low information diet."[39] But most of them won't make that choice. Your friends who choose to continue feasting at the all-you-can-eat information buffet will willingly, naturally, and unknowingly curate information for you. Please let them.

PRACTICE 2: STOP SWIMMING IN INFINITY POOLS

Not ready for the extreme approach of practice 1? Then consider this more moderate tactic: stop swimming in "infinity pools," which Google veterans Jake Knapp and John Zeratsky define as "apps and other sources of endlessly replenishing content."[40] Infinity pools

---

*The cat's out of the bag now. Let's see how many of my friends get this far in the book. :)

include Instagram Stories, the Facebook News Feed, and news web-sites designed to make it easy to seamlessly scroll from one irrelevant story to the next.

What's the alternative to infinity pools of content? *Finite* pools of content. Instead of scrolling endlessly through CNN online, subscribe to a finite news roundup. There are many podcasts and email newsletters that fulfill this purpose. You can find links to some of the best at JordanRaynor.com/RYT.

At the risk of sounding like a ninety-year-old, here's another idea for choosing finite over infinite content: read *physical* magazines and newspapers. The beauty of these products is that there is a clear beginning and end. You *can't* scroll infinitely. In the words of the *New York Times* masthead, it's "all the news that's *fit* to print" (emphasis added).[41]

Of course, it's much harder to find finite pools to swim in on social media. If you're committed to keeping social media in your life, consider setting time limits for it, especially on your phone. But be careful here: time-limiting features still rely on self-control, and the temptations of these social media apps are *crazy* difficult to resist.

With all infinity pools, swim at your own risk. There's no lifeguard on duty, and it is far too easy to drown in the never-ending noise.

PRACTICE 3: CHOOSE MORE FILTERED CONTENT

It's not just *finite* information sources that help us turn down noise—*filtered* content does as well. The fact is that some forms of media have more gatekeepers and filters in place than others, ensuring that the noise that gets through has a higher likelihood of being relevant, accurate, and high quality.

Take books, as an example. An author has to first get an agent to represent her book, then a gatekeeper at a publishing house has to decide whether it's worth publishing, and then a team of editors puts the manuscript through the wringer. Of course, these people help ensure that what's being written is accurate and high quality, but most importantly, they all have to decide *that the words are worth saying*. And even if that team decides to publish a book, in order for you to even *hear* about it, a friend has to be convinced it's good enough to recommend.

What's my point? At least a dozen people have to decide a book is important before it gets into your hands. Compare that to podcasts, Instagram, or BuzzFeed, where the only filter is the click of a button, the swipe of a thumb, or the pop-up of an ad promoting the next story. To be clear, too many books can create just as much noise as other mediums. But at least books are *filtered* for accuracy and importance, making it much more likely they'll be useful to you and the work God has called you to focus on.

Of course, just as there is no such thing as finite content on social media, there's also no such thing as filtered content on it. That's why we have to quit or confine social media, which brings us to our next practice.

PRACTICE 4: RENOUNCE OR ATTAIN INDEPENDENCE FROM SOCIAL MEDIA

I won't argue against the position that social media adds value to our lives. But as with everything else, "Is this thing valuable?" is the *wrong* question to ask. The *right* question is "How *much* value does this thing offer me and at what *cost*?"

You probably find Netflix valuable, but would you pay a thousand dollars each month for it? Of course not, because value is always relative to cost. We must conduct cost-benefit analyses with everything that might increase the noise in our lives. Paul's words about food in 1 Corinthians are helpful here: "All things are lawful for me, but not all things are *profitable*" (6:12, NASB). The wisest time redeemers don't ask,

"*Can* I keep this app on my phone?" They ask, "*Is it profitable* to keep this app on my phone?" Is social media valuable? Yes. But as we've seen, the cost of social media is also exorbitantly high.

After running the cost-benefit analysis for yourself, you may decide to quit social media altogether. Personally, I've decided to take a different approach, best articulated by the famous rabbi Abraham Joshua Heschel: "The solution of mankind's most vexing problem will not be found in renouncing technical civilization, but in attaining some degree of independence of it."[42]

I decided years ago that social media was valuable enough to keep in my life, but given the tremendous power it wields, I also decided to "attain some degree of independence" from it. How? By confining *when* and *where* I check it.

I check just two social media apps once a day for a few minutes after my kids go to bed. But my decision of *where* I check them may be even more important.

With the exception of the two apps on my phone, I have confined 100 percent of my social media usage to my desktop computer. The simple step of deleting these infinity pools from my mobile device has made a world of difference in minimizing the noise in my life and helping me go deep at work and home. When I first made this move, I still spent time on these services in my desktop browser, but because of the inferior experience on desktop relative to mobile, over time I just gave up. Yes, I still have accounts on the major social media platforms, but it is *exceedingly* rare that I personally check them. Confining social media to your desktop is like a nicotine patch that slowly but surely reduces your addiction to these services.

Unless you're a professional social media manager, I can't urge you strongly enough to renounce or "attain independence" from social media. The status quo isn't working. Our lives are too noisy, and if we want to discern and do our most exceptional work for the glory of God and the good of others, we need space to reflect and think.

PRACTICE 5: PARENT YOUR PHONE

Researchers at the University of Chicago have found that your ability to concentrate suffers simply by having your smartphone in the room with you, even if your phone is on silent or turned off![43] And as author Andy Crouch pointed out, "The mere presence of your smartphone in your pocket is a nudge, a gentle reminder that just a tap away are countless rewards of information, entertainment, and distraction."[44]

That's why I put my phone to bed around seven thirty every night and keep it in its metaphorical room until seven the next morning—two hours after I wake up. I need significant time away from the noise and anxiety my phone produces, especially in the morning, when I am spending time in God's Word and trying to listen to his voice.

Our phones have unbelievable power for good and for evil. If we care about our ability to cultivate time of silent reflection in the model of Jesus, we must exert more control over our mobile devices. In the words of John Mark Comer, you must "parent your phone."[45] That's a great way to think about it. Just as you would with your kids, *you* decide what time your phone will go to bed and what time it will be allowed out of its proverbial room. *You're* the parent in this relationship.

But wait, Jordan, didn't you say in chapter 2 that we need our Commitment Tracking System with us at all times to capture open loops? And didn't you recommend our CTS be an app on our phone? Yup. There are two easy ways to solve this. First, you can use a pen and paper to jot down open loops while your phone is in bed. The next day, you can quickly type these items onto the Inbox List in your CTS. Second, if you're using OmniFocus as your CTS, you can easily integrate it with a voice service such as Alexa.*

Okay, the five practices we just walked through will help you significantly cut out the noise in your life. But what do you do with all

---

*You can learn how in the free video at JordanRaynor.com/RYT.

your newfound silence? The following four practices answer that question, making space for you to think, be creative, go deep, be at peace, and listen to God's voice.

PRACTICE 6: GET COMFORTABLE WITH THE CREVICES OF YOUR DAY

If you follow some of the first practices in this chapter, you're going to find yourself with slivers of silence you didn't have before. The first thing I recommend doing with your newfound solitude is nothing—*absolutely nothing.*

The next time you find yourself waiting for the elevator at work, resist the urge to unlock your phone. The next time you finish reading a chapter of a book five minutes before your kids are expected home, don't turn the page. The next time you hop in your car to run a ten-minute errand, don't press play on that podcast episode (yes, even if it's mine).

As we've seen, boredom doesn't come naturally for us in the twenty-first century, so we have to intentionally develop the *skill* of being bored. Start small by refusing to fill the cracks and crevices of your day with noise.

Start small by refusing to fill the cracks and crevices of your day with noise.

PRACTICE 7: TAKE A WALK

It seems as though every religion has a corresponding physical discipline. "Hinduism has yoga. Taoism has tai chi. Shintoism has karate. Buddhism has kung fu."[46] You get the point. But is there a physical discipline for Christianity? Pastor Mark Buchanan suggested there is: walking. In his book *God Walk,* Buchanan pointed to God's walks in the Garden of Eden (see Genesis 3:8) to argue that we worship "the three-mile-an-hour God."[47]

For centuries, some of the most productive Christians have practiced the godlike discipline of walking to listen to his voice as well as their own thoughts. In seminary, Dr. Martin Luther King Jr. walked an hour every day.[48] The nineteenth-century theologian Søren Kierkegaard spent nearly every afternoon walking the streets of Copenhagen. "I have walked myself into my best thoughts," he said, crediting the practice.[49] As William Wilberforce fought to end slavery, he took "many long walks" to think and restore his soul.[50] C. S. Lewis "thought and walked and read and walked and sometimes even wrote and walked, making up lines in his head and then stopping for a while to write them down in a notebook. [Lewis] walked for exercise of both mind and body."[51]

The fact that these wildly productive Christ followers valued walking so much should command our attention. But if anecdotes aren't your thing, consider the science, summarized nicely in Ryan Holiday's *Stillness Is the Key:*

> A study at New Mexico Highlands University has found that the force from our footsteps can increase the supply of blood to the brain. Researchers at Stanford have found that walkers perform better on tests that measure "creative divergent thinking" during and after their walks. A study out of Duke University found a version of what Kierkegaard tried to tell his sister-in-law, that walking could be as effective a treatment for major depression in some patients as medication.[52]

I mentioned earlier that while I was CEO of Threshold 360, I came to the conviction that the number one skill a founder or CEO can have is the ability to separate the essential from the noise. During my time at Threshold, my favorite practice for prioritizing my to-do list was walking. Every morning, I would leave the office and walk to my favorite coffee shop downtown. I wouldn't look at my phone. I would just walk alone in total silence. I would just *think*. I'd ask, *Out of everything competing for my attention right now, what actually matters? What's the highest-leverage use of my time today?* I credit those walks with helping my team and me to focus on the right things and build a great company.

Today, as I lead the team at Jordan Raynor & Company, I continue to walk almost daily—well, run actually. But my runs aren't primarily about exercising my body; rather, they are meant to exercise my mind. I run to think, to make creative connections, and to listen to where God might be leading this movement. On nearly every run, I put half a dozen substantial ideas onto my Inbox List (see chapter 2) or gain clarity on something that wasn't clear before. In fact, as I was outlining this chapter, I got pretty stuck, so I went for my morning run. In twenty minutes, I figured out what I had spent the previous ninety trying to sort out in front of my laptop. Mark Buchanan is right: "Walking opens doors that sitting only strains against."[53]

If I'm traveling to your city and you see me in the streets walking by myself, talking to myself, don't worry. Contrary to appearances, I'm not crazy—I'm just embracing the silence and solitude to hear myself think.

PRACTICE 8: WRITE TO THINK

As I mentioned before, I always wrap up episodes of my podcast by asking guests to leave our audience with a single piece of advice on how to do their most exceptional work for the glory of God and the good of others. One surprising answer to that question came from Luke LeFevre, the chief creative officer at Dave Ramsey's company, Ramsey Solutions.

Given LeFevre's experience as a serious executive leading a team of more than a hundred people, I expected him to share some advice about hiring, management, or creativity. Instead, he encouraged our audience to take up the practice of journaling. He said, "You have to get to a place where you're writing what you actually think to God and giving yourself space to actually be quiet."[54]

I'm not a daily journaler like LeFevre, but I can attest to the value of "writing what you actually think." When I am in need of clarity, nothing does the trick better than writing out my thoughts in full prose—not bullet points, but full-on sentences.

The magic of journaling is why Amazon doesn't allow employees to use PowerPoint decks in internal meetings. From early on, the company's founder, Jeff Bezos, required employees to "write six-page narratives laying out their points in prose, because Bezos believes doing so fosters critical thinking."[55] Of course, in many ways a memo is just a more corporate form of journaling. President Eisenhower took a similar approach, employing the regular practice of thinking by writing to make sense of complicated decisions and tame intense emotions.[56]

Author Julia Cameron said that journaling is the equivalent of spiritual "windshield wipers."[57] I think that's right. Are you having trouble hearing your own thoughts or the voice of God? Turn down the noise, pick up a pen (or laptop), and start writing.

PRACTICE 9: PUT THE QUIET BACK IN QUIET TIME

As we saw in chapter 1, immersing ourselves in God's Word daily is *the* keystone habit for redeeming our time. But as I mentioned before, most of these quiet times aren't all that quiet. Reading the Word is still a form of consuming information. Doing so is, of course, critical to *hearing* God's voice, but if we want to *listen* to God's voice and connect the Word to what's going on in our work, lives, and souls, we need to still our minds. We need to "*be still,* and *know* that [God is] God" (Psalm 46:10).

Yes, I'm talking about literally just sitting there, in front of the Word, and doing *nothing*—for one, three, five minutes, whatever. Just sit and meditate on what you just read, allowing the Spirit to connect the dots from the Word to your heart. I vote that we make quiet times a little quieter again. Who's with me?

COLLECTING THE PUZZLE PIECES

In chapter 2, you collected everything you have *any* commitment to doing in the future in your Commitment Tracking System (CTS). But we all know that not all to-dos are created equal. Some things matter much more than others. Now that you've dissented from the kingdom of noise, you finally have the mental space to decide what matters most. Why is prioritizing our to-do lists so important, and how can we do it well? That's the piece of the puzzle we'll pick up in the next chapter.

CHAPTER 4

PRIORITIZE YOUR YESES

To redeem our time in the model of our Redeemer, we must decide what matters most and allow those choices to prioritize our commitments.

Finding a note that reads, "One day I'll be in the NBA," on a seventh grader's bathroom mirror is not at all unique. But when that seventh grader is a *girl*—well, that's a different story.

A tweenage Tamika Catchings was discussing professional goals with her family, when someone asked her what it was that she really *loved* to do. As Catchings shares, "My answer didn't take hours of deep thought or soul searching like some kids' did. My response was almost immediate."[1] Catchings wanted to play professional basketball.

There was only one problem: the Women's National Basketball Association (WNBA) didn't exist at the time, and no woman had ever played in the all-men's NBA. Catchings said,

> But that wasn't stopping me. I had every confidence that I could play in the NBA. With the guys. . . .
>
> Claiming basketball as a profession seemed so natural. I sat down and wrote my goal on a piece of paper: "One day I'll be in the NBA." I didn't write, "I'll be in the NBA despite the fact that I'm a girl." No, I wrote, "One day I'll be in the NBA." Period.[2]

Catchings pinned her audacious goal on her bathroom mirror. "Every day when I woke up that's the first thing I saw," she said. "I looked in the mirror and saw my dream, my goal, right there, and it became more achievable, more attainable, day by day."[3]

Defining such a clear and ambitious goal empowered Catchings to prioritize her time and to-do lists. She had a clear and compelling yes that inspired her to say no to lesser things that were competing for her time and attention. "Basketball became another kind of homework," she said. "If I wasn't at an official team practice . . . I was outside shooting hoops. That was my routine. Every day. Even during the summer, I was up at seven or seven thirty in the morning and rushed through breakfast so I could get to the court."[4]

Once she was in college, the NBA announced that they would be commissioning the WNBA, bringing professional women's basketball to the United States. "'One day I'll be in the NBA' was now a possibility in a way I hadn't imagined," Catchings shared. "My goal had changed to 'One day I'll be in the WNBA.'"[5]

Not only did Catchings achieve her refined goal, but she went on to have one of the most impressive careers in the history of sports, appearing in more WNBA playoff games than any other player, becoming the only woman to appear in ten WNBA All-Star Games, and earning four Olympic gold medals, making her one of only three American basketball players—*male or female*—to ever accomplish that feat.[6]

"By the grace of God and through a lot of hard work, my dreams became my reality," Catchings shared.[7] But she's careful to add that achieving her dreams isn't what matters most. What matters is "to excel in the thing God wants you to do and made you to do."[8]

Amen. Whether we're basketball players, entrepreneurs, designers, working moms, woodworkers, or writers, what matters is doing our most exceptional work for the glory of God and the good of others. But to do that, we must redeem our time. And to redeem our time, we need to get crystal clear on what matters most on our never-ending to-do lists. We must clarify what we're saying yes to so we can say no to nonessential things along the way. That's Tamika Catchings's story. It's also the story of Jesus Christ.

A PURPOSE HARDER THAN STEEL

When you study the Gospels through the lens of trying to understand how Jesus stewarded his time, one glaring truth jumps off the pages: Jesus was *crazy* purposeful. In the words of the great Dorothy Sayers, "Under all his gentleness there is a purpose harder than steel."[9] Nobody in Jerusalem had more things competing for their attention, yet Jesus always seemed to be able to discern the essential from the noise.

No passage of Scripture illustrates this better than Mark 1:29–38. After driving out some evil spirits at the synagogue, Jesus healed Peter's mother-in-law and a bunch of her neighbors. Understandably, the town's residents wanted more healing from Jesus the next day. But Jesus said no. Why? Because he had already committed his time to a bigger yes. In response to the people's request for more of his time, Jesus said, "Let us go somewhere else—to the nearby villages—so I can preach there also. *That is why I have come*" (verse 38).

> *Jesus understood his purpose, and that allowed him to take the long list of things he could do and pare it down to the things he knew he should do to finish the work the Father gave him to do.*

Jesus understood his purpose, and that allowed him to take the long list of things he *could* do and pare it down to the things he knew he *should* do to finish the work the Father *gave* him to do (see John 17:4). And with his work prioritized, Jesus focused relentlessly. Pastor Kevin DeYoung pointed out that

Jesus knew the difference between urgent and important. He understood that all the good things he *could* do were not necessarily the things he *ought* to do. . . . If Jesus had to live with human limitations, we'd be foolish to think we don't. The people on this planet who end up doing nothing are those who never realized they couldn't do everything.[10]

Man, that's good. Yet again, Jesus's example leads us to a timeless biblical principle for redeeming our time today. Here it is:

PRINCIPLE #4
PRIORITIZE YOUR YESES

To redeem our time in the model of our Redeemer, we must decide what matters most and allow those choices to prioritize our commitments.

The fact is, not all yeses are created equal. Not every to-do carries equal weight in doing good works for others. If you're familiar with the 80/20 Principle, you know what I'm talking about. "The 80/20 Principle asserts that a minority of causes, inputs or effort usually lead to a majority of the results, outputs or rewards."[11] Even if you've never read that formal definition before, you have undoubtedly experienced the 80/20 Principle many times, as it is one of the most powerful laws of the universe: for example, 80 percent of your stress comes from 20 percent of your clients, 80 percent of volunteer hours at church are given by 20 percent of the members, and 80 percent of time spent on Disney+ comes from 20 percent of the platform's content (if my household has anything to say about it, the *Frozen* franchise). In other words, although everything may *look* equally important, it's not. Not even close. Author and speaker John Maxwell said it best: "You cannot overestimate the unimportance of practically everything."[12]

I don't have to hammer this point home any further. You get it. No one's questioning whether the 80/20 Principle is real. Your experience tells you it's as real as the earth is round. The more interesting question for those of us who care about redeeming our time is this: How can we, like Jesus, identify the work that matters most and ignore everything else?

First, as we saw in the previous chapter, we must create space for silent reflection. But solitude alone isn't enough. We must also grasp the truth that we have the power to choose what matters most rather than allowing others to choose for us. Let's face it: most people operate under the assumption that the opposite is true. *My priority is whatever pops up in my email inbox or whatever fire breaks out at work today.* Most people are *reactive* rather than *proactive* with their time and priorities.

To be clear, some of this is good. If your boss tells you that something is important, it's important and you need to do it. That's a way of serving your boss and the Lord well (see Ephesians 6:5–8). But spending *all* your time in reactionary mode is not the way of Jesus. To redeem your time in the model of your Redeemer, you must develop the habit of identifying what matters most on your to-do list at any given point in time.

The six practices in this chapter are going to help you do just that. But before we begin, I'd like for you to picture a five-story building. In chapter 2, we walked in from the street onto the first floor of this metaphorical building, collecting our open loops, defining our work, and creating comprehensive lists of projects and actions. We started on the first floor for a reason: you can't prioritize your to-do list until you've made an exhaustive list of your to-dos. The problem now, of course, is that the number of items on your to-do list (or Commitment Tracking System) is overwhelming, and as we've started to explore in this chapter, not all those to-dos are created equal. Some of them matter much, much more than others. The question is, which ones?

Now that we've dissented from the kingdom of noise in chapter 3 and created some space to think, we can finally start to answer that question. But to do so, we need to take the elevator up to the fifth floor of our metaphorical building and work our way floor by floor back to where we started. Here's a map of where we're going and the questions we will be answering as we step out onto each floor:

5TH FLOOR: Mission (Why do you exist?)

4TH FLOOR: Callings (Which roles will you choose to carry out your mission?)

3RD FLOOR: Long-Term Goals (What do you want for each of your callings?)

2ND FLOOR: Quarterly Goals (How will you make progress toward your long-term goals in the next three months?)

1ST FLOOR: Projects and Actions (What are the items on your to-do list that will help you accomplish your quarterly goals?)

BASEMENT: Posteriorities (What must you avoid at all costs to accomplish your quarterly goals?)*

Yes, you counted correctly. There are *six,* not five, levels listed here. But just as in a real building, the basement doesn't deserve to be called a floor. Like basements, posteriorities must be kept out of sight and out of mind for reasons that will become clear in just a few minutes. Okay, let's get on the elevator and head to the top floor.

PRACTICE 1: ACCEPT YOUR MISSION

There are entire books that teach you how to write a life mission statement to define the purpose of your life. I'm going to let you off the hook and give you permission to take those books off your reading list. Matt Perman explains why: "Most time management books treat your mission statement as something you define for yourself. But in reality, defining your mission isn't in the arena of things you decide. . . . Your mission is discovered, not chosen."[13] Pastor and author Rick Warren put it this way in *The Purpose Driven Life:*

The search for the purpose of life has puzzled people for thousands of years. That's because we typically begin at the wrong starting point—ourselves. . . .

*If you find this visual helpful, visit JordanRaynor.com/RYT to download the "5 Floors of Priority" worksheet with space to write your answers to these questions as you work through the chapter.

Contrary to what many popular books, movies, and seminars tell you, you won't discover your life's meaning by looking within yourself. . . . You didn't create yourself, so there is no way you can tell yourself what you were created for![14]

We don't get to define our mission in life. Our Creator does. And what does our Creator say our mission is? In short, *his glory*. You see this mission all throughout Scripture, perhaps most succinctly in 1 Corinthians 10:31, where Paul said that in "whatever you do, do it all for the glory of God."

The mission of your life is to glorify God. Period. Full stop. Highlight that. Write it down. *That's your why*—your North Star. In the words of *Mission Impossible,* this *is* your mission—your only choice is whether or not you will accept it.[15]

The mission of your life is to glorify God.
Period. Full stop.

Now, *how* do we glorify God? The list of answers to that question is long, but as we saw in chapter 1, one of the primary ways we bring God glory is by doing "good works" for others (see Matthew 5:16, ESV; Ephesians 2:10). How do we do the maximum number of good works for others? By redeeming our time—by being purposeful, present, and wildly productive.

Got it? Good. Hop back on the elevator and let's take it down to the next floor.

PRACTICE 2: CHOOSE YOUR CALLINGS

MISSION
CALLINGS
LONG-TERM GOALS
QUARTERLY GOALS
PROJECTS & ACTIONS
POSTERIORITIES

Although our mission in life is *discovered,* our callings are *chosen.*

As we saw in chapter 1, God has invited you to be a part of his massive kingdom-building mission, and that mission is the same for each of us. But in his great grace, our heavenly Father has given us a tremendous amount of freedom to choose exactly how we will contribute to that mission. And guess what? As long as you are obeying his commands, you can't make a wrong decision. Proverbs 19:21 says, "Many are the plans in a person's heart, but it is the LORD's purpose that prevails." Commenting on this verse, Timothy Keller said, "In a sense, for a Christian, there is no 'plan B.' "[16]

Of course, we should be diligent and wise as we seek to choose our callings and where we spend our time, but the fact that we can't make a "wrong" decision frees us from analysis paralysis. God's sovereignty gives us the courage to simply make a choice. At the end of the day, regardless of which callings we choose, vocational or otherwise, the Lord's purposes *will* prevail. His plans *cannot be thwarted* (see Job 42:2).

Believer, you are *free* to choose the callings you think you can fulfill most exceptionally well for the glory of God and the good of others. So yes, take time to explore your options. But at some point, *you've just got to make a choice,* because kingdom work is getting done and you want the blessing of being part of it.

Personally, I have chosen three primary callings: husband, father, and entrepreneur (more specifically, CEO of Jordan Raynor & Company). That's two familial callings and one vocational. That's it.

If you know what your callings are, write them down on the "5 Floors of Priority" worksheet that accompanies this chapter.* If

---

*You can download the worksheet at JordanRaynor.com/RYT.

you need help choosing your callings, I'd encourage you to read my book *Master of One*. Can't afford it? Email me at hello@jordan raynor.com and I'd be more than happy to send you a copy. Choosing your callings is an important decision, and I want to help you choose well.

After you've accepted your mission and chosen your callings, it's time for us to descend another level in our metaphorical building to set epic long-term goals for each of our callings.

PRACTICE 3: SET EPIC LONG-TERM GOALS

Every Broadway-show writer knows that a great musical starts with a catchy "I want" song. In *The Little Mermaid,* Ariel wanted more.* In *West Side Story,* Tony wanted Maria. In *Hamilton,* Alexander wanted his shot. To redeem our time, we need to learn to metaphorically sing our own "I want" songs. It's not enough to define our high-level mission and callings. To prioritize our to-do lists, we must clearly articulate what we want for each of our roles that's in line with God's mission for the world.

Over the past fifty years or so, the veracity of this wisdom has been proven an overwhelming number of times: 90 percent of more than a thousand studies have shown that productivity is significantly enhanced by articulating what we want in the form of "well-defined, challenging goals."[17] In this practice and the next, I'm going to show

---

*Let's face it: "Part of Your World" in *The Little Mermaid* is the greatest "I want" song of all time. The inimitable Lin-Manuel Miranda agrees: "Lin-Manuel Miranda on 'I Want' Songs, Going Method for 'Moana' and Fearing David Bowie," *Dinner Party,* February 10, 2017, www.dinnerpartydownload.org/lin -manuel-miranda.

you a simple method for setting "well-defined, challenging goals" that will help prioritize your to-do list. In this practice, we will focus on setting *long-term* goals for each of our callings.

Some people refer to long-term goals as "vision statements," but to me that sounds lame, corporate, and helplessly vague. I prefer to call them "Big Hairy Audacious Goals (BHAGs)," the term Jim Collins and Jerry Porras coined in their classic book *Built to Last*.[18]

What is a BHAG? Exactly what it sounds like. Rather than define it further, let's look at some examples. Tamika Catchings's BHAG was to play in the NBA. William Wilberforce's BHAG was to abolish the slave trade. At the organizational level, NASA's BHAG in the 1960s was to put a man on the moon. Google's BHAG is to "organize the world's information."[19]

If you're an entrepreneur, your BHAG might be getting to ten million dollars in annual revenue in the next five years. If you're a mother, your BHAG could be to see your kids walking with the Lord when they go off to college. If you're a graphic designer, your BHAG could be getting promoted to chief creative officer by the time you're thirty-five.

In practice 2, I shared each of my callings. Here are the BHAGs I have defined for each:

- Husband: love Kara as Christ loves me
- Father: inspire Ellison, Kate, and Emery to be joyfully engaged in God's mission for the world
- Entrepreneur: inspire and equip every Christian to do their most exceptional work for the glory of God and the good of others

As you can see, some BHAGs are *eternal* (e.g., Google's "organize the world's information"), while others are *time bound* (e.g., seeing your kids walking with the Lord before they go off to college). Either works, as long as your BHAG is *big* enough, *challenging* enough, and *inspiring* enough to bring focus to your to-do list.

As you think through what your BHAGs might be for your personal and professional callings, I'd encourage you to pray and think big—*epically* big. Why? Here are five reasons.

FIVE REASONS TO SET MORE EPIC GOALS

#1: God Has the Power to Do "Immeasurably More" Than We Can Imagine

Bill Gates has observed that "most people overestimate what they can achieve in a year and underestimate what they can achieve in ten years."[20] In my experience, that's exactly right. When thinking about long-term goals, we are capable of accomplishing far more than we think—well, not us exactly, but God working *through* us. Ephesians 3:20 makes this clear: "[God] . . . is able to do immeasurably more than all we ask or imagine, according to his power that is at work within us." God's power is at work within you, believer. Through the Holy Spirit, you have the Creator God dwelling inside you. And Jesus said that through the Spirit, *we* "will do even greater things" (John 14:12) than *he* did during his time on earth as we rely less on our strength and more on his. That truth should lead us to set *wildly* audacious goals at work and home.

#2: Big Goals Are Easier to Achieve Than Small Goals

Most people don't believe that God is able to do "immeasurably more" than they can imagine, so they aim for average. This creates a fascinating paradox: because nearly everyone aims for average-sized goals, the level of competition *decreases* as the size of your goal *increases*.

The level of competition decreases as the size of your goal increases.

In my experience, it's easier to raise a million dollars in venture capital than a hundred thousand dollars. It's easier to get national press than local press. It's easier to land an internship at the White House than at a local ad agency.

The story behind that last one really sticks out in my mind. When I was a public relations student at Florida State, most of my classmates had a tough time landing internships, largely because they were all competing for the same spots at local advertising and communication agencies. I set my eyes on a far more audacious goal—landing an internship at the White House—and by the grace of God alone, I landed it. But do you know what? My fellow White House interns were no more remarkable than my classmates at Florida State. They were simply more audacious. They set bigger goals.

Peter Drucker, widely regarded as one of the greatest management thinkers of the twentieth century, once said, "It is just as risky, just as arduous, and just as uncertain to do something small that is new as it is to do something big that is new."[21] That's spot-on. Set your own goals accordingly.

#3: Big Goals Make It Easier to Say No

Wish you were better at saying no to requests for your time and attention? Welcome to the club. In chapters 5 and 7, I'll say a lot more about how the Christian approach to saying no should differ from the world's, but for now, I'll leave you with this simple insight: it is much easier to develop the habit of saying no if you're challenged and inspired by what you've already said yes to.

Can you grab a cup of coffee? "No, I'm sorry. I'm on a tight deadline, and I have to finish this draft today to stay on track." *I'm in town for* *the night. Can you meet up for dinner?* "Wish I could, but I'm fully committed to taking my kids to Awana at church."*

New York Times columnist David Brooks said, "If you want to win the war for attention, don't try to say 'no' to the trivial distractions you find on the information smorgasbord; try to say 'yes' to the subject that arouses a terrifying longing, and let the terrifying longing crowd out everything else."[22] Yes! A "terrifying longing." *That's* what you're after as you set your Big Hairy Audacious Goals. But before you set your BHAGs, here are two more reasons to pray for bigger vision for your goals.

#4: Big Goals Recruit Others to Your Cause

Brett Hagler is the CEO of New Story, a nonprofit with one of my favorite BHAGs: "building a world without homelessness."[23] When I spoke with Hagler on my podcast, I asked him to talk about the value of setting audacious goals like that one. His answer was priceless: "Bold ideas attract bold people."[24]

If you lead an organization, you know that recruiting the right people to your team is priority number one. Top-tier talent doesn't want to work on boring problems—*they want to change the world.* Setting bigger goals will help recruit the world's best talent to your cause.

But it's not just leaders of organizations who can benefit from this advice. If you set a big goal of landing a book deal, you'll inspire your friends to help you share your ideas with the world. If you're a stay-at-home dad, setting bigger goals for your family has the power to inspire your wife and kids to follow your lead. Again, bold ideas and goals attract bold, talented people to follow.

---

*By the way, the phrase "fully committed" has become a favorite of mine. More on why in chapter 7.

#5: *You're Unlikely to Fail Entirely*

Google cofounder Larry Page said that "the thing that people don't get" about setting big goals is that "even if you fail at your ambitious thing, it's very hard to fail completely."[25] If you set a Big Hairy Audacious Goal and fail, you will likely have made more progress than you would have if your aim had been more "realistic." Big thinking produces big results.

But even if we *do* fail entirely and fall flat on our faces, the gospel of Jesus Christ ensures that we are secure. In success or failure, "we know that in all things God works for the good of those who love him, who have been called according to his purpose" (Romans 8:28). We may not see that "good" on this side of eternity, but God will be faithful to this promise, which enables us to take bigger swings for his glory and the good of others.

What do you sense the Lord leading you to desire over the next few years or decades of your life? What will your "I want" song be for each of your callings? If you need time to explore your options, by all means, take it. But if you know your BHAGs, write them on your worksheet. Now let's hop back on the elevator and take it down to the next floor of our metaphorical building, where you'll get even more practical, setting "well-defined, challenging goals" that will prioritize your to-do list over the next three months.

PRACTICE 4: DRAFT QUARTERLY GOALS

BHAGs answer the question "What do I want?" But we need another tool to answer "How are we going to get there? And how will we measure progress to ensure we're on track?" To bring focus and order to our to-do lists, we need to set goals on a regular basis (I would argue quarterly) that bring us a few steps closer to our BHAGs.

But let's face it: traditional goal-setting tools can feel lame and unmotivating. Maybe you've set key performance indicators (KPIs) or SMART goals at work. These tools may lead to results, but they are hardly inspiring. Why? Because they often fail to connect results to inspiring objectives. I don't know about you, but I need goals that are inspiring *and* measurable.

That's why I love objectives and key results (or OKRs), made famous by Google, whose leaders credit the goal-setting framework with "changing the course of the company forever."[26] You read that right: Google, one of the most valuable and respected companies in history, credits a *goal-setting framework* for its historic success. Oh yeah, and Google is not the only one. Over the years, the list of companies and individuals to adopt the OKR framework is so impressive that it's almost laughable: Bono, Disney, Amazon, Netflix, and Wikipedia are just a few.*

So, what exactly *is* an OKR?

There are two components: an *objective* (the *O* in OKR) and a set of corresponding *key results* (the KRs).

According to John Doerr, the renowned venture capitalist who literally wrote the book on OKRs, "Objectives are significant, concrete, action oriented, and (ideally) inspirational."[27] They are what need to be achieved in a given period of time to move you closer to achieving your BHAGs.

Key results are "specific and time-bound, aggressive yet realistic. Most of all, they are measurable and verifiable."[28] In the words of former Googler and Yahoo! CEO Marissa Mayer, "It's not a key result

---

*You can hear the chief operations officer of Wikimedia Foundation, Janeen Uzzell, and I geek out about OKRs on my podcast. The episode link can be found at JordanRaynor.com/RYT.

unless it has a number."[29] Key results are *how* you will know if you have accomplished your objective.

Objectives and key results combine to create this simple goal formula: "I will [objective] as measured by [key results]." In a given quarter, you should have one to five sets of objectives, each with one to five corresponding key results.*

Let's look at a couple of examples to make OKRs concrete. Remember our example of the graphic designer whose BHAG is to be promoted to chief creative officer by the time she turns thirty-five? Let's pretend that one of the barriers to our designer's career progression is a lack of management experience. To make progress toward her BHAG this quarter, our designer might draft a set of OKRs that looks like this:

> Objective: Gain the management experience I need to move closer to being chief creative officer
> - *Key Result #1: Convince my boss to allow me to hire one direct report next year*
> - *Key Result #2: Meet with three chief creative officers to get advice on how to best position myself for this role*
> - *Key Result #3: Complete an online course on managing creative talent*

As you can see, "objectives and key results are the yin and yang of goal setting—principle and practice, vision and execution. Objectives are the stuff of inspiration and far horizons. Key results are more earthbound and metric-driven."[30]

Let's look at another example to see why it's so important to have

---

*Why the constraint? Because you can remember and do only so much in a given three-month period. For more on the genius of this, check out the free video on this topic at JordanRaynor.com/RYT.

both the "inspiration" of objectives and "metric-driven" key results. Let's say you have a full-time job and also sell online courses on the side. You want to focus on your course business full time, but today the economics of doing so just don't make sense. Here's a set of OKRs you might set for this quarter:

> Objective: Be in a financial position to focus on my course business full time
> - *Key Result #1: Sell one hundred units of my flagship course*
> - *Key Result #2: Hold calls with three past students to pick their brains on what other courses they'd like me to teach*
> - *Key Result #3: Go from $25,000 to $40,000 cash on hand*

Selling a hundred units of any course isn't easy. If that's one of your key results for this quarter, there are going to be days in which the work feels like a grind. But a quick glance at your objective will remind you why you're working so hard. You're doing it because it is a means to a more meaningful end: focusing full time on the work you believe God has called you to do!

I hope these examples demonstrate why it's critical to marry aspirational goals with measurable ones. An inscription inside an eighteenth-century church explained it best: "A vision without a task is but a dream; a task without a vision is but drudgery; a vision and a task is the hope of the world."[31]

Now, you might be saying, *Jordan, OKRs look like something big companies do. I'm a freelancer. Does this apply to me?* Absolutely. OKRs are for all who care about focusing their to-do list on what matters most and making substantial progress toward their Big Hairy Audacious Goals. I started using the OKR framework when I ran a large team, but when I stepped down as CEO to focus on writing full time, I continued to use the OKR framework when I was a team of one. You can too.

But, Jordan, I already have goals at work that my employer sets for me. Why would I set OKRs? Because you have goals for your career and life that your current employer isn't going to help you track. If you work for someone else, your first professional priority is to serve your employer through the ministry of excellence (see Colossians 3:22–25). But that doesn't mean you can't set personal goals for your career and life outside of work. My advice is simple: execute the goals your employer hands you with excellence and draft OKRs to help prioritize your personal time.

And yes, I find a ton of value in setting OKRs for each of my callings, including my roles as husband and father. If you're curious to see some of my personal OKRs, check out the corresponding video at JordanRaynor.com/RYT. At that link, you'll also find a video that provides a step-by-step guide to setting your own OKRs the very first time.

PRACTICE 5: REFINE YOUR PROJECTS LIST AND ACTIONS LIST

We're back on the ground floor of our building, where we return to our functional to-do lists: the Projects List and Actions List we created in our Commitment Tracking System (CTS).

In chapter 2, I encouraged you to add anything "urgent or distant that you have *any* level of internal commitment to doing in the future" to your CTS. This is critical for ensuring that your brain is free from the pressure of open loops, but this also creates a conundrum in that your Projects List and Actions List are now filled with many things you want to keep track of outside your brain but that aren't going to be priorities anytime soon. So, how do you focus these lists on the items that matter most without losing track of everything else?

The first step is making the projects and actions you're committed to working on this quarter visually distinct. If you're using a paper-based to-do list or CTS, this can be as simple as highlighting the items on your Projects List and Actions List you're committed to working on over the next three months. If you're using a digital CTS, you can make your priorities visually distinct by flagging or starring items related to your goals for the quarter or by separating your Projects List and Actions List into subfolders. This latter approach is my personal preference. In my CTS, the projects and actions I'm committed to working on over the next three months are in a folder labeled "This Quarter." Where are all my other commitments stored? I haven't deleted them. I have placed them in a separate physical space, effectively locking them in the basement of my mind. That critical habit brings us to the final practice in this chapter.

PRACTICE 6: LOCK POSTERIORITIES IN THE BASEMENT

One day, Warren Buffett was asked for some career advice by one of his employees, a guy named Mike Flint. Buffett encouraged Flint to make a list of his top twenty-five career goals. When Flint showed him the list, Buffett asked him to whittle it down to only five items. When Flint presented the revised list to his boss, he agreed to focus on his new top five goals that he'd circled, but that he'd still work on the other twenty items, as he had time, because they were still important to him. Here's what Buffett said in response: "No. You've got it wrong, Mike. Everything you didn't circle just became your Avoid-At-All-Cost list. No matter what, these things get no attention from you until you've succeeded with your top 5."[32]

Flint's top five goals were his *priorities*. What Buffett was encouraging him to avoid at all cost are what Peter Drucker called "posteriorities."[33]

From the more than one hundred interviews I've conducted with some of the world's most effective Christians, I've come to believe that one of their greatest skills is their ability to keep posteriorities on hold until their priorities are accomplished. Like Jesus, these people are just as deliberate about what they're saying no to as what they're saying yes to. Randy Alcorn, the pastor and absurdly productive writer, calls this "planned neglect."[34] I *love* that.

> *One of the greatest skills of the world's most effective Christians is their ability to keep posteriorities on hold until their priorities are accomplished.*

Personally, when I am feeling overwhelmed, it's usually not because I've failed to delegate properly. Nearly every item on my to-do list is something I should personally be doing but simply don't have enough time to do. The problem is that I've committed to doing too many things *at once*. I've defined too many priorities and not nearly enough posteriorities.

To redeem our time and focus fully on the work God has created us to do, we need to develop the habit of locking our posteriorities in the basements of our minds. This is part of the reason why I love the five-story picture I've been building throughout this chapter. To the people living or working in our metaphorical building, it's a five-story structure. Nobody would call it a six-story building, because the sixth floor—the basement—is out of sight and out of mind. That is precisely the way we should treat our posteriorities.

How practically can you do this? In practice 5, I showed you how to make your priorities for the quarter visually distinct on your to-do list or CTS. Now I want you to put *everything else* in a separate physical space. Again, if you're using a paper-based to-do list or CTS, this could be as simple as highlighting your priorities and leaving your posteriorities unhighlighted. But for me, that's not enough. I need my posteriorities to be out of sight in order for them to be out of mind. That's why I place all the priorities on my Projects List and Actions List in a "This Quarter" subfolder and put everything else—my posteriorities—in a "Someday" folder.*

Organize your to-dos however you'd like. But given our perennial temptation to spread ourselves thin and fail to model Jesus's relentless focus, I *beg* you to do whatever it takes to keep your posteriorities in the basement of your mind and to-do list.

If you hit your OKRs before the end of the quarter, by all means feel free to take new projects out of the basement so you can do more good works for the glory of God and the good of others. But until those goals are hit, you have to keep the posteriorities locked away.

In a previous company I ran, my business partner and I would hold "stop doing" meetings every two weeks to review each other's to-do lists and recommend dropping projects that weren't in line with our OKRs. That was an invaluable practice for focusing our time on what mattered most. If you have a spouse, close friend at work, or business partner, I would encourage you to do something similar: share your goals and invite the individual to question whether or not the items on your to-do list are aligned with your priorities.

COLLECTING THE PUZZLE PIECES

We've come a long way in just a few chapters, collecting the first four pieces of the puzzle to redeeming our time. Now that we've started with the Word, collected our commitments, dissented from the kingdom of noise, and prioritized our yeses, we're ready to pick up the fifth piece of our proverbial puzzle: learning what it takes to be fully present and focused on our priorities each day.

---

*For a deeper look at how I organize my personal CTS, check out the video on this topic at JordanRaynor.com/RYT.

CHAPTER 5

ACCEPT YOUR "UNIPRESENCE"

*To redeem our time in the model of our Redeemer, we must accept our
unipresence and focus on one important thing at a time.*

The famous writer C. S. Lewis was an eccentric guy. He refused
to drive a car or read the newspaper.[1] He made up his own
rules for Scrabble.[2] And he drank pints of beer before noon
with J. R. R. Tolkien.[3] Reading biographies of this beloved author,
one can't help but see parallels to Benedict Cumberbatch's portrayal
of Sherlock Holmes: utter genius with a not insignificant number of
idiosyncrasies.

Perhaps the most eccentric chapter of Lewis's story was his relationship with a woman named Janie Moore. During WWI, Lewis
developed a friendship with Moore's son, Paddy, and before the
friends went off to war, they made a pact: if either should die in battle,
the survivor would look after the deceased's family.[4] After Paddy
was killed in France, Lewis made good on his promise. Upon being
discharged after a war injury of his own, Lewis returned to England
and moved in with Janie Moore (whom he called "Mrs. Moore") and
her daughter, Maureen.

His relationship with Mrs. Moore was complex, to say the least.
It's clear that Moore filled a void in Lewis's life caused by the death
of his own mother when he was only nine years old. But a few of his
biographers suggest that Lewis's relationship with the mother of his
former best mate may have been romantic.[5] Perhaps this is why Lewis
developed a habit of fudging the truth about Moore's true identity,
telling his friends in Oxford that she was merely his landlady.[6]

Romantic speculation aside, what's clear is that Moore played a pivotal and largely positive role in Lewis's life for many years. At one point, Lewis was so fond of the Moores that he privately referred to them as his family, even though Lewis's father was still very much alive.[7]

But the honeymoon with his surrogate family didn't last forever. Over the years, Mrs. Moore became more of a burden than a joy, making it exceedingly difficult for Lewis to redeem his time. As Lewis's stepson and biographer recounted, "All day everyday there were endless little jobs" that Mrs. Moore would ask Lewis to do.[8] He'd be writing a chapter of his next book, when Mrs. Moore would urgently summon him to wash a dish or mop the floor. Seemingly in an attempt to draw attention to herself, Moore was always inventing crises, running Lewis "ragged trying to look after her."[9] His biographer further explained,

> [Lewis] would be writing or studying in his room when he would suddenly hear a terrible crash from somewhere down-stairs and a plaintive cry from Mrs. Moore. In great anxiety he would run down to find that she had tripped over something and was not in the least hurt but very "shaken." [Lewis] would bustle about setting all to rights again and then return to his work, only to be summoned again ten minutes later to go out and buy something or to perform some other minor and largely unnecessary task.[10]

The fact that Lewis accomplished any meaningful work during these years is nothing short of a miracle. Yet according to multiple biographers, Lewis never once complained. Even though Mrs. Moore was undoubtedly a thorn in his side, Lewis's love of Jesus led him to extend sacrificial mercy, fulfilling his duty *for more than thirty years* until Moore's death, shortly after her health had forced her into a nursing home.[11]

Then Lewis's productivity *exploded*. With Mrs. Moore gone, he "was able to work solidly and uninterrupted for hours at a time and . . .

[was] able to establish a routine. . . . He was able to plunge into his work now that there were no tiresome distractions at home."[12] In the six years after Moore left his home, Lewis published *ten* books, including the titles that continue to account for the lion's share of his book sales today: *Mere Christianity* and all seven volumes of the Chronicles of Narnia.

For the first time in his career, Lewis was experiencing regular opportunities for deep work. Cal Newport, a professor of computer science at Georgetown University, made this concept famous in his terrific book *Deep Work: Rules for Focused Success in a Distracted World*. Newport defined deep work as "professional activities performed in a state of distraction-free concentration that push your cognitive capabilities to their limit."[13]

As the life of C. S. Lewis so vividly illustrates, the ability to cultivate depth at work is *incredibly* valuable. One prolific business writer called it "the superpower of the 21st century."[14] Sound extreme? I don't think so. In fact, I couldn't agree more. I believe the discipline of deep work is the single most important practice in my day-to-day pursuit of mastery. I find the habit so valuable that when I served as CEO of Threshold 360, we included this concept in our core values, saying that "deep work makes the dream work."*

How is deep work connected to redeeming our time? It is the key to doing more good works in the same twenty-four-hour time constraint. According to the legendary Peter Drucker,

> Doing one thing at a time means doing it fast. The more one can concentrate time, effort, and resources, the greater the number and diversity of tasks one can actually perform. . . .
>
> This is the "secret" of those people who "do so many things" and apparently so many difficult things. They do only one at a time.[15]

* Hat tip to *Reading Rainbow*'s LeVar Burton.

Concentration. Focus. Depth. Those are *the secrets* to being wildly productive.

But, of course, depth isn't just valuable at work. It's equally, if not more, valuable at home. Think back to the last time you had true quality time with your spouse, kids, or friends. I can almost guarantee that depth was a precondition. Your phone was stored away or at least not buzzing every three minutes. The TV was off. There was nobody competing for your attention. You were fully present, fully focused, and fully engaged. In other words, you were going deep with a single important thing or person.

Given that our ability to go deep has great value at work *and* at home, allow me to offer a broader definition of *depth* that extends beyond Newport's definition of *deep work*.

DEPTH: the ability to focus intensely on one important thing at a time

As we've seen, the ability to cultivate depth is valuable to *you*, but more importantly your ability to go deep at work and at home is valuable to *others*. The way you serve your employer well is by being fully present, doing focused work that yields tremendous output. The way you serve your family well is by being fully present physically *and* mentally when you're at home. In today's distracted world, being fully present is one of the most valuable presents you can give.

> *In today's distracted world, being fully present is one of the most valuable presents you can give.*

Author and speaker Michael Hyatt said, "We call it *paying* attention for a reason! Focus is valuable."[16] And I would argue that focus is *increasingly* valuable precisely *because* it is increasingly *rare*. In the words of the great philosopher Taylor Swift, "Important, rare things are valuable."[17] That's true of music, but it's even more true of depth.

The resource most at risk of becoming extinct in our generation isn't water or oil—it's our ability to focus.

I don't need to bombard you with a million studies to prove this point. You and I both know that our ability to focus is under attack every single day. But I do wonder if we fully appreciate the gravity of this problem and just how dangerous distractions are to our attempts to redeem our time and execute the goals we set in chapter 4. According to psychologists at the University of London, distractions negatively influence our intelligence *twice as much as marijuana.*[18] And there's a scientific explanation as to why. It's called "attention residue."[19]

Let's say you sit down to write a blog post. You're thirty minutes into the project and you're starting to get into a groove, when all of a sudden you receive an email from your boss, who's checking in on a different project. Your focus and train of thought has been broken, and even if you don't reply, part of your attention is still on the email and what it represents. Rather than thinking solely about the blog post, you're now wondering, *Did I schedule enough time to work on that other project this week?* or *I hope my boss isn't upset that I haven't completed it yet.*

This is attention residue, and according to researchers, it is disastrous to productivity. Not only does it take time for you to refocus on the blog post, but as one researcher said, "People experiencing attention residue after switching tasks are likely to demonstrate poor performance on that next task."[20] In other words, it's going to take you *longer* to finish the blog post, *and* your draft won't be as high quality as it would have been had you not been distracted.

Again, this isn't just a problem at work. Let's say you're at home on a Saturday, playing with your kids, when you sneak a peek at your email. You see a message that came in late Friday night that you know is going to blow up your calendar next week. As we learned in chapter 2, jotting down a reminder of an open loop that the message represents will help. But if it's a particularly anxiety-inducing or exciting message, it could cause you to be mentally absent all weekend, even if you're physically present. I've learned this one the hard way more than once.

How can we fight back against distractions that gunk up our brains with attention residue? How do we, like Jesus, stay focused on one important thing at a time in our modern world? Before we can answer those questions, we need to more clearly identify the enemies in our fight for depth because they're not as clear-cut as they might seem.

FIVE ENEMIES IN THE FIGHT FOR DEPTH

Enemy #1: External Distractions

To cite the cliché of all clichés, "We are more connected than ever before," which is just another way of saying that we're more *distracted* than ever before. You know what I mean: emails, texts, notifications from social media and mobile games, phone calls, your boss popping into your office, your daughter wanting to play pretend while you need to be on a conference call. You get it.

There's no doubt that external distractions are enemy #1 in our fight for depth. The good news is that this is often the easiest enemy to combat, as we'll see in the practices in this chapter. But before we get to those, we need to acknowledge four *internal* enemies that keep us from going deep.

Enemy #2: Fake Productivity

The opposite of deep work is shallow work, which Cal Newport defined as "noncognitively demanding, logistical-style tasks, often performed while distracted."[21]

Shallow work includes email, administrative tasks, and most meetings. *Some* shallow work is important. If you want to serve your boss well, you have to respond to her emails. If you want to get reimbursed for expenses, you have to submit an expense report.

But *most* shallow work is *not* important. At all. So why do we do so much of it? Because shallow work is *much* easier than deep work. Let's face it: spending a whole day in meetings and checking emails is easier and less exhausting than sitting in a chair for two hours and focusing intensely on creating something new. Shallow work makes us look and feel productive without having to make any significant effort. Spending all day in the shallows leads to what we might call "fake productivity": work that makes us look busy but is terribly unimportant and fails to move us any closer to our goals.

> *Spending all day in the shallows leads to what we might call "fake productivity": work that makes us look busy but is terribly unimportant and fails to move us any closer to our goals.*

The temptation to opt for fake over actual productivity is real. Sin has ensured that, by default, we are all lazy. Given a choice between an easy path that makes us *look* busy and a hard path that actually gets results, most people will choose the easy path. But not you and me. Why? Because we believe God has given us work to do! We're not here to just coast through life. We are here on a mission to glorify God by doing as much good for others as possible.

Enemy #3: Quick Highs

It's no secret that social media companies design their products to be addictive. Sean Parker, the founding president of Facebook,* is quoted as saying,

> The thought process that went into building these applications, Facebook being the first of them, . . . was all about: "How do we

---

*Perhaps better known as Justin Timberlake in *The Social Network*.

consume as much of your time and conscious attention as possible?" And that means that we need to sort of give you a little dopamine hit every once in a while, because someone liked or commented on a photo or a post or whatever.[22]

By the way, that "dopamine hit" comment wasn't metaphorical. It wasn't a slip of the tongue. Scientists have proven that unpredictable rewards (e.g., whether or not there will be a new like) *actually* release dopamine in our brains, much like smoking or pulling the lever on a slot machine.[23] In a characteristically over-the-top monologue, comedian Bill Maher said, "Let's face it, checking your 'likes' is the new smoking. . . . Philip Morris just wanted your lungs. The App Store wants your soul,"[24] and, by extension, your ability to cultivate depth at work and home.

But before we throw stones at the attention economy conglomerates, we need to humbly recognize that *we actively seek out* these quick highs throughout the day, and not just from social media services. Maybe for you it's checking the news ten times a day or picking up your phone to see if you have a new text. Authors have been known to incessantly check their bestseller rankings on Amazon (or so I've heard). My current addiction is checking download numbers on my podcast. On my worst days, I'll check our latest metrics three to five times. And here's what's *certifiably crazy* about my behavior: my podcast downloads are almost perfectly predictable. I *know* roughly what those numbers are going to be before I check them. And oh by the way, even if there were an anomaly and I saw a huge spike in downloads, that fact would have almost no impact on my ability to make progress on my projects and goals. All it does is distract me from my work or spending time with my wife and kids. It's why I call distractions like these "crack stats." They are addicting but unsubstantial and unfulfilling.

Almost everyone I know is addicted to some flavor of a digital quick high. For now, be cognizant of what yours is. We'll put this enemy in its place in just a minute.

Enemy #4: Savior Complex

Let's face it: many of the distractions in our lives make us feel important. We might complain about receiving a hundred emails a day or constantly being interrupted by our teams or having to wade through *so* many Instagram notifications, but part of us *loves* these things. They make us feel needed. They make us feel important. They make us feel like the hero and the savior of our small corner of the universe. I know because *I can be this guy*. If you ever hear me complain about how many emails I receive, what I'm *really* trying to say is, "Look at how important I am!" You have permission to slap me in the face.

A savior complex is a powerful motivator to stay addicted to the things that distract us from depth. But remember, as Christ followers, our importance and significance come from one place: our unmerited adoption as children of God, *not* the number of unread emails we complain/brag about. So stop using these distractions as a means of boosting your self-worth. Remember who you are in Christ, and get back to depth for his glory and the good of others.

Enemy #5: Makeshift Omnipresence

In *The Social Network,* Aaron Sorkin's classic film chronicling the rise of Facebook, we watch Mark Zuckerberg being deposed against his will. The opposing attorney, sensing that Zuckerberg is mentally absent, asks, "Mr. Zuckerberg, do I have your full attention?" To which Zuckerberg replies, "No. . . . You have *part* of my attention. You have the minimum amount" (emphasis added).[25]

Arrogant? Sure. Refreshingly honest? You bet. The truth is that most of the people and projects in our lives have only part of our attention due to the four enemies we've already been introduced to as well as this fifth and final one: our misguided attempts to be in two (or three or four) places at once.

In study after study, the scientific community continues to prove that multitasking is a myth. So why do we still do it? Why do we still believe it's possible?

First, it could be because we've failed to articulate a "terrifying longing" that can capture our full attention. If that's you, go back to chapter 4 and do the work of defining your goals and prioritizing your to-do list. Life's too short to spend time on things that deserve only half our attention.

Life's too short to spend time on things that deserve only half our attention.

Second, for those of us who *have* set clear and compelling goals for our lives and work, we'd be wise to recognize that our temptation to multitask might stem from that deep-seated desire that began all the way back in the Garden of Eden—namely, to play God. This leads to what Jen Wilkin called our "makeshift omnipresence."[26]

Now more than ever, our world offers the illusion that we can be fully present in more than one place at a time. But it's just that: *an illusion.* You know how I know? *Because we're not God,* and even when God himself came to earth in human form, he traded in his godly *omni*presence for the human *uni*presence you and I experience today.

OMNIPRESENT GOD, UNIPRESENT JESUS

Jesus had to deal with many of the same challenges we face today as we seek to redeem our time, including frequent distractions that competed for his attention.

A man literally threw himself at Jesus's feet as Jesus was walking down the road (see Mark 10:17). A woman touched Jesus's cloak, distracting him with the knowledge that he had healed her (see 5:27–30). One time, a man literally dropped through the roof over Jesus's head as Jesus was preaching (see Luke 5:17–19). Has anyone ever dropped through the roof above your desk while you were working? If not, you're not more distracted than Jesus was.

In contrast to secular wisdom that encourages us to issue a blanket "no" to these sorts of distractions, there were times in which Jesus welcomed them (more on this in chapter 7). But other times, Jesus made significant effort to eliminate distractions and cultivate depth. One of my favorite examples of this comes from Matthew 12:46–50:

> While Jesus was still talking to the crowd, his mother and brothers stood outside, wanting to speak to him. Someone told him, "Your mother and brothers are standing outside, wanting to speak to you."
>
> He replied to him, "Who is my mother, and who are my brothers?" Pointing to his disciples, he said, "Here are my mother and my brothers. For whoever does the will of my Father in heaven is my brother and sister and mother."

Given that the main point of this passage is Jesus's words about who is and who is not his family, it can be easy to miss the fascinating "B story." Jesus was working, "talking to the crowd," doing the work the Father sent him to do—namely, preaching the gospel of the kingdom. All of a sudden, his family showed up. They were waiting outside. *And Jesus ignored them.* When Jesus was told that his family was waiting, he didn't say, "That's all, folks. My family's here. You know the rule: God first, family second, work third!" He continued teaching. In that moment, he was called to work, and he remained fully focused and present with the task at hand.

Conversely, when he was with his family and friends, he was fully focused on *them*. In Mark 9, we see Jesus coming off a hard day's work with his disciples. Verses 30–31 say, "They left that place and passed through Galilee. Jesus did not want anyone to know where they were, because he was teaching his disciples." Once his work was done,

Jesus was intentional about being fully focused on his twelve closest friends.

If Jesus couldn't be in two places at the same time, neither can we.

In these and many other encounters in the Gospels, Jesus was reminding us that God is omnipresent and we humans are not. When omnipresent God "became flesh" (John 1:14), Jesus embraced the human limitations of being unipresent. If *Jesus* couldn't be in two places at the same time, neither can we. Like Jesus, we must learn to "choose our absence,"[27] which brings us to the fifth principle we need in order to redeem our time.

PRINCIPLE #5
ACCEPT YOUR UNIPRESENCE

To redeem our time in the model of our Redeemer, we must accept our unipresence and focus on one important thing at a time.

Before we jump into the practices that outline how to do this in our modern context, I want to warn you that you *can* lose your ability to cultivate depth and focus. Tony Schwartz, CEO of the Energy Project, explained it this way: "The more we allow ourselves to be distracted, the more diminished our capacity for absorbed attention becomes over time. Much like an unused muscle, our attention grows weaker and shorter with disuse."[28]

Focus is like a muscle of the mind: work it out and depth will develop; ignore it and it will atrophy. In other words, when it comes to the skill of focusing your attention, you can choose to use it or lose it.

As we've seen, there are powerful enemies fighting against our efforts to model Jesus's commitment to depth. If we don't do the work of wrestling those enemies to the ground, we can *permanently* lose our ability to focus. So let's get to it!

PRACTICE 1: TAKE CONTROL OF WHEN YOU CHECK MESSAGES

I want you to imagine something. Instead of delivering mail to your home once a day, the mailman has started making deliveries *one hundred* times a day. And he no longer stays at the curb. With each delivery, he rings your doorbell and you get up from whatever you're doing, open the door, take the piece of mail, and open it (or, at a minimum, steal a glance at who sent it). That would be *insane,* right? Yet that is exactly how many people treat email and text messages.

You will *never* be able to go deep at work or home until you believe this truth: *you have more control than you think over when you respond to incoming messages.* Underline that. Highlight it, *even if you don't believe it yet.* My prayer is that by the end of this section, you will.

As we've already seen, the number one enemy in our fight for depth is external distractions, and more specifically, email, text messages, and social media notifications—in short, incoming messages that command your immediate attention. In a minute, I'm going to show you my method for checking these messages at only one to three predetermined times each day. But given how radical and countercultural this practice is, I want to address three common objections to this idea *before* I show you how to implement it.

Objection #1: People Expect Me to Respond to Their Messages Immediately!

This may be true, but that doesn't mean it's sane. And in my experience, the perception that people expect immediate responses is oftentimes not reality.

Do you know what happened when I stopped checking text messages with every new ping and confined my responses to a few times a day? Nothing. My friends and colleagues didn't say a thing. I think some of them were *relieved* from the pressure of the never-ending volleying of texts that sapped their *own* ability to cultivate depth throughout their day.

One study found that a quarter of people feel obligated to answer messages immediately.[29] But again, this perception is not always reality. I know *plenty* of people—bosses included—who don't share this expectation. Remember, your boss has a boss too. Even if your supervisor is the CEO, he or she reports to a board of directors. Most bosses don't want to be enslaved to email any more than we do.

The expectation I communicate to my team is that every message should be responded to within one business day. If you lead any number of people and are looking to *dramatically* increase the quality and speed of their work, I'd encourage you to communicate something similar. Here's a script you're free to tweak and make your own:

> It has come to my attention that some of you assume that I expect near immediate responses to the emails and other messages you receive from me. I'm sending you this email to let you off the hook: you have up to one full business day to respond to my messages.
>
> I know how hard it is to get meaningful work done when you feel that you need to be responding to emails and Slack messages all day. I hope this new, clearer policy encourages you to keep those messaging apps closed for longer stretches of time so you can get deeper, more meaningful work done.

Not blessed with a boss who will send you that email? Don't worry, I'm going to give you your own script to send to your supervisor and other VIPs in just a minute. But first we need to overcome two more common objections to controlling when you respond to incoming messages.

Objection #2: I'm Afraid I'm Going to Miss Something Urgent!

In the heat of war, Napoleon waited *three weeks* before opening any of his mail. When he finally did crack open his letters, he would laugh at how many seemingly urgent, important things had miraculously resolved themselves.[30]

My point? Although many things look urgent, almost nothing is. That email asking you to send over a PowerPoint? It can likely wait a few hours. That text from a friend asking where you're meeting for coffee tomorrow? It can wait.

But, Jordan, you don't understand. I'm in sales! I'm in customer service! I'm a pastor! My job is to respond quickly. It's true that some jobs require more responsiveness than others. But virtually *no* job requires *constant* responsiveness. You likely require *some* amount of depth to do your job well. If you've ever shut down your email or turned off your phone to knock out an important report or pitch deck, you've proven my point.

It isn't necessary to spend cumulatively less time processing incoming messages in order to cultivate depth. But it *is* necessary to exert more control over *when* you spend time in the shallows.

And because I most frequently hear this objection from salespeople, let me say this: I have spent most of my career as a sales-focused CEO in businesses where the mandate was to grow revenue 50 percent a quarter. And do you know how I got that job done? Not by responding to every email the moment it came in, but by doing the opposite and deliberately delaying communication so I could focus deeply on every proposal, pitch, and customer interaction.

Objection #3: I Need the VIPs in My Life to Be Able to Get Ahold of Me!

This is the most valid objection to the idea of checking your messages only a few times a day. I'm right there with you on this one. I want my wife, parents, investors, and team to be able to contact me anywhere, anytime. And the system I am about to recommend to you accommodates that. Let's dig into that system now.

STEP 1: CHOOSE YOUR TIMES

The first step to taking control over when you check your emails, texts, and other messages is simply choosing the times you will check them in a typical day. And for now, let's stay focused on workdays.

Currently, I check messages once a day, but there have been periods of time in which I have checked messages as many as three times a day. In my opinion, checking messages more than three times a day is unnecessary for the vast majority of roles, but if you're able to convince yourself that you're an exception, feel free to schedule more than three. Again, what's more important than the *number* of times you check your messages is that *you choose* when you will check them.

> *What's more important than the number of times you check your messages is that you choose when you will check them.*

When should you check your messages? I *strongly* recommend you do so after at least one block of deep work (more on these blocks in practice 3). Why? Because checking messages requires far less energy than deep work, so it's inefficient to check them when your energy is highest. We'll take a closer look at this in chapter 7 and physically draw blocks of time for checking messages on your calendar. At this point, all I'm asking you to do is commit to this first step of predetermining when you will check your messages.

STEP 2: BUILD YOUR VIP LIST

We all have people in our lives whom we want to be available to at all times. Take a minute right now to make a list of who those people are—your VIPs, if you will. My list of VIPs includes:

Personal

- *My wife*
- *My kids' school*
- *My extended family (mom, dad, brother, grandparents, and in-laws)*
- *Five of my closest friends*

Professional

- *My assistant*
- *My agent*
- *The three members of my team I am actively working on projects with (this list changes as projects come and go)*
- *My investors*

Once you've built your list of VIPs, I recommend that you give them unfettered access to you on the device they're most likely to contact you on when they need you urgently: your phone. Both iOS and Android devices allow you to add your VIPs to a list that will ensure these people and these people only can reach you when your phone is on Do Not Disturb. Go ahead and add your VIPs to your list of "Favorites" (iOS) or "People" (Android) on your phone. Not sure how to do this? Check out the guides on "How to Enable the Do Not Disturb Feature" at JordanRaynor.com/RYT.

STEP 3: SET CLEAR EXPECTATIONS

It's easy to assume that everyone responds to messages the same way you do, but of course that's not true. To serve the people in your life well, you can't just suddenly go from responding to messages imme-diately to responding every few hours. Once you've chosen your times for checking messages and built a list of your VIPs, you need to *proactively* set expectations for when and how your VIPs can get ahold of you. The message you send to do this will look slightly different based on who you're sending it to. Here's an example of a message you might send to VIP colleagues and team members:

> In an effort to better serve you and my work, I've decided to check email only three times each workday at 10:30 a.m., 1:00 p.m., and 4:30 p.m. EST.
>
> If your message is urgent, please call me at 123-456-7890.
>
> Thank you for understanding!

And here's a version you can text to your VIP friends and family:

> Hey there! I'm trying to be more focused at work and home, so I'm going to start keeping my phone on Do Not Disturb. That means I will be checking my text messages only a few times a day. I've added you to the "Favorites" list on my phone, so if you need me, please call me. Your call will always come through, and if I'm available, I'll answer.

What about people who aren't on your VIP list? How do you communicate expectations with them for when you will respond to their messages? Personally, I don't think you need to be proactive here. Depending on the nature of your interactions with people outside your VIP list, you may not need to say anything at all. But I recommend that if you do decide to set expectations with non-VIPs that you include some version of the script above in an email auto-responder or in your email signature.

I know the idea of setting expectations like this might freak you out, especially if you're considering sending some variation of these

messages to your boss. But remember, bosses don't want to be responding to emails every five minutes either. Trust me, they likely got to
their positions precisely because they have found a way to cultivate
depth. For what it's worth, if I saw an email like this from a member
of my team, I would be *ecstatic* and looking for every opportunity to
give that person more responsibility because I know that depth is the
silver bullet for effectiveness. Still not fully comfortable with making this change? Consider reframing the script above as a one-week
experiment rather than a permanent policy.

Depth is the silver bullet for effectiveness.

PRACTICE 2: ELIMINATE EXTERNAL DISTRACTIONS

With message checking confined to predetermined slots on our calendars, we can now start eliminating external distractions. Again, these
are enemy number one in our fight for depth. Proverbs 4:25 tells us,
"Fix your gaze directly before you." This practice is how we will do
that at work and home.

At Work

PHONE CALLS

Now's the time to turn on the Do Not Disturb feature on your mobile
phone. This will send all calls to your voice mail except those from
your VIP list. Again, if you're not comfortable going all in with this
change, consider making this a one-week experiment.

TEXT MESSAGES

Although Do Not Disturb can ensure that text messages don't buzz
you the moment they come in, texts can still cause an enormous
amount of attention residue if you let them show up on the lock screen

or notification center of your phone. I don't let them. I don't even have the badge turned on to show me how many unread text messages I have. I have to open the text messages app on my phone to see if there are any unread messages. And let me tell you, making that change has been one of my most game-changing habits. Thank you to John Mark Comer's *The Ruthless Elimination of Hurry* for this tip![31]

EMAIL

If you implemented practice 1, there's no need to keep your email open anymore. Close out of the application entirely. *But, Jordan, I need to access my email to do deep work.* I get it. I often do too, which is why I'm going to share the simplest and one of my all-time favorite productivity hacks. Years ago, in Gmail (my preferred email service), I entered a search for this phrase: "No way an email matches this search query." That search generated a unique URL, which I then bookmarked in my browser. Now if I ever need to search for something in my email, I just click that bookmark, which opens up Gmail with zero messages matching my search, and thus no messages competing for my attention. Seriously, this hack is a *game changer*. And it takes less than one minute to implement, as you can see in the video I've shared at JordanRaynor.com/RYT. At that link, you'll also find videos showing you how to replicate this trick in other email clients.

DESKTOP APPLICATIONS

Email isn't the only application on your computer that creates distractions. Close out of *any* applications that don't need to be open for the project you've chosen to focus on. And while you're at it, disable notifications from all your desktop apps, as some are able to "push" notifications even when they're closed.

CALENDAR

This is going to sound like a minor thing, but I find it incredibly helpful: instead of having my calendar show my entire week, I have it show only the present day. This helps ensure I'm not distracted by what's coming up tomorrow or later in the week. Jesus said, "Do not worry about tomorrow, for tomorrow will worry about itself. Each day has enough trouble of its own" (Matthew 6:34). Keeping one calendar day in front of me at a time helps me live this out in a very practical way.

BROWSER

For goodness' sake, for your own good, *please* close your seventeen browser tabs. You can focus on only one project at a time, so stop volunteering to be distracted by other concerns. In speaking with people who have this habit, I've learned that open browser tabs often represent open loops—reminders of things they need to do. If that's you, go back to chapter 2, practice 3, to extract the open loops from your browser tabs and close them for good.

SMARTWATCH

If you have one and want to cultivate depth, dumb it down using the same features and functionality you'd use on your phone.

WORK SPACE

It's hard to focus on one thing at a time when there are physical things competing for your attention. If you executed practice 3 in chapter 2, you've already taken care of this problem. If you haven't, go back to that practice now that you have a stronger motivation—namely, the pursuit of depth. Make sure everything in your work space (Post-it Notes, folders, books, and so on) belongs "where it is, the way it is."[32]

AUDIO

Audible distractions at work can be significant, especially if you work in an office with other people. When I was CEO of Threshold 360, the walls of my office were *paper* thin. I could hear every word spoken in the offices to my left and right. That's when I made one of the best purchase decisions of my life and bought a pair of noise-canceling headphones. Demonstrating my commitment to our core value that "deep work makes the dream work," I even approved the purchase of the same headphones for our employees. Who knows? Your employer might too.

At Home

For years, I was extremely disciplined about eliminating external distractions at work, but when I got home, it was a different story. I took my phone off Do Not Disturb and spent much of the evening distracted by text messages and push notifications. By the grace of God, I eventually realized how ludicrous it was that I was committed to depth at work but not at home. As Christ followers, we are compelled to pursue excellence in each of our callings. And excellence at home requires time, attention, and focus—in other words, depth. Remember, it's not just deep *work* we're after but a deep *life*. Like Jesus, we want to be fully present with whatever important task or person we've chosen to give our attention to in a given moment.

> *As Christ followers, we are compelled to pursue excellence in each of our callings.*

I strongly recommend that once you transition from your office to your home (or, for those of us who work from home, from upstairs to downstairs or den to living room) you physically put your laptop and phone away—out of sight and out of mind. Here's why. If you're like me, then you spend a lot of time with your family and friends after a full day at work. Of course, this is when your finite source of willpower is most depleted, making it the hardest time of day to resist the temptation to be distracted by your digital tools. Maybe you can resist the temptation to check email, text messages, and Instagram while your kids are trying to tell you about their day, but ashamedly I cannot. The only way I can be fully present and focused on my family is if my laptop and phone are completely out of sight and out of mind.

When I end my workday at 5:00 p.m., I leave my laptop in my office and put my phone in our master bathroom and keep it on silent. The goal is to not touch my phone from 5:00 p.m. to 7:00 p.m. (my kids' crazy-early bedtime—don't judge). At 7:00 p.m., I check my text messages (*not* email) one last time, check a few to-dos off my personal to-do list in OmniFocus, and glance at Timehop, Instagram, and any "crack stats" I really want to check before I end my day. And then I put my phone to bed, giving me an hour to an hour and a half to be fully present with my bride.

I know this habit sounds impossible to some of you, especially if your boss or team members frequently call you after hours. When I was CEO of Threshold 360, I experienced the same pressure. That's why I tweaked this habit a bit during those years. I still kept my phone in our master bathroom between five and seven, but I turned the ringer on, ensuring that if the VIPs in my life really needed me, they could get my attention. This effectively converted my mobile phone into a landline for a couple of hours each evening. If someone really needed me, they could reach me. Otherwise, the temptation to be distracted had been eliminated.

PRACTICE 3: SCHEDULE DEEP-WORK APPOINTMENTS WITH YOURSELF

You're used to scheduling appointments with *other people*. But to cultivate depth—especially at work—you're going to have to get used to scheduling appointments with *yourself*. Why? Because to make progress toward the goals you defined in chapter 4, you are going to need long stretches of uninterrupted time.

Depth requires two ingredients: focus and time. In the previous two practices, I showed you how to quiet external distractions and cultivate focus. Now we need to take a closer look at the second ingredient, which is time.

Once again, here's Peter Drucker: "To be effective, every knowledge worker . . . needs to be able to dispose of time in fairly large chunks. To have small dribs and drabs of time at [your] disposal will not be sufficient even if the total is an impressive number of hours."[33] Drucker was pointing out what you've likely already experienced to be true—namely, that it takes time to really get in the groove of a meaningful project.

To understand this better, we can look to the science of sleep. For decades, scientists have understood that it takes long periods of uninterrupted time for a sleeping person to enter REM sleep. Sleep cycles predictably last for about ninety minutes, beginning with lighter, NREM sleep and then working up to REM. If you wake up in the middle of a cycle, your body is forced to start all over again. The same appears to be true with work.

If you read my previous book, *Master of One*, you'll recall my writing about the 10,000-Hour Rule, made famous by Malcolm Gladwell in his book *Outliers*. The rule states that 10,000 hours of purposeful practice is the key to mastering any skill, with purposeful practice distinguishing itself from naive practice in a few ways, one of which is intense focus.[34] In the study that catapulted the 10,000-Hour Rule to fame, researchers studied a group of violinists to understand what distinguished the most exceptional performers from the average ones. The answer? Two things: the top violinists got nearly an hour more of sleep per night than their less masterful counterparts, and they practiced without interruption or distraction for—wait for it—*ninety minutes at a time*.[35]

Just as we need time to go deep in our sleep, we need long stretches of uninterrupted time to go deep in our work. Of course, we're not just going to "find the time" to do this; we must be proactive about *making* the time on our calendars by scheduling appointments with ourselves to do deep work.

How much time should you schedule? Ninety minutes seems to be the sweet spot, so that's a great goal. But I realize that's not realistic for everyone. If you're starting from nothing, adding just thirty minutes of depth to your day will help you make *significantly* more progress toward your goals.

Remember, focus is a muscle. It builds over time. Start small and "add more weight to the bar" as your focus muscle develops. But I'll warn you: the more you work this muscle out, the more you will *want* to work this muscle out. Once you experience the magic of depth, it's addicting. You (and others) will be blown away by how much more you get done in the same amount of time just by giving yourself the time and focus to go deep.

When should you schedule deep work? Whenever your energy is highest. Just like a muscle, the ability to focus and cultivate depth gets fatigued throughout the day.[36] This explains why more than two-thirds of catastrophic plane crashes happen during the last phase of flight.[37] Most people's energy is highest in the morning, but not everyone's (more on this in chapter 7). Schedule your blocks of deep work for when your energy is highest.

Is there a maximum amount of deep work you can do in a day? There is. Again, we all have a finite amount of willpower in a given day; thus, there's a cap on how long we can focus intensely at our desks. Most scientists believe this cap is four hours in a twenty-four-hour time period.[38] In my experience, that's about right. As you'll see in chapter 7, I budget five and a half hours of deep work every workday, but due to meetings and other demands on my time, I rarely end up spending that much time at the deep end of the pool. When I do, I am utterly exhausted at the end of the day.

So, if you can get only four hours of deep work done in a given workday, what do you do with the rest of your time? That question brings us to our next practice.

PRACTICE 4: CREATE SPACE FOR THE SHALLOWS AND SERENDIPITY

If you executed practice 1, you've already created space for one type of shallow work: checking email, texts, and other messages. Once you've scheduled deep-work appointments with yourself, consider leaving the rest of your day open for other shallow activities: meetings, calls, checking your "crack stats," and dealing with any interruptions that popped up during your blocks of deep work. With dedicated space on your calendar to respond to those interruptions, almost everything can be ignored for a few hours, enabling you to stay focused on the deep task at hand.

With dedicated space on your calendar to respond to interruptions, almost everything can be ignored for a few hours, enabling you to stay focused on the deep task at hand.

Let's say your admirable goal is to get four hours of deep work done before lunch. Your Time Budget template (which we will build in chapter 7) might look something like this:

- Deep Work: 8:00–9:30
- Break: 9:30–9:45
- Deep Work: 9:45–11:15
- Check Messages: 11:15–11:30
- Deep Work: 11:30–12:30
- Lunch: 12:30–1:00
- Shallow Work: 1:00–4:30

Let's pretend your boss calls you at 10:00 a.m., right after you've started your second block of deep work. She wants to know if you have ten minutes to discuss tomorrow's meeting. According to your calendar, you have more than four hours of time budgeted for shallow work after 1:00 p.m., making it easy for you to say something along these lines: "I'm happy to chat right now, but I'm actually in the middle of drafting that proposal you requested and I'm really in a groove. I could stop and talk about the meeting now, or I could call you back at one. Which would you prefer?"

A message like this is respectful and reasonable, and it forces the trade-off decision onto your boss. More often than not, your boss will tell you to call her later, allowing you to get back to depth. By not scheduling every second of your day, you'll have time to confine and respond to interruptions like these that will inevitably pop up as you try to focus on your most important work.

Like in the hypothetical schedule above, I get four hours of deep work done before lunch nearly every day. I estimate that more than 80 percent of the value I create happens during those four hours. The second half of my day is much choppier as I go in and out of shallow activities such as meetings, calls, email, and tasks that don't require a lot of time or energy. Look at the chart of how I spent my day

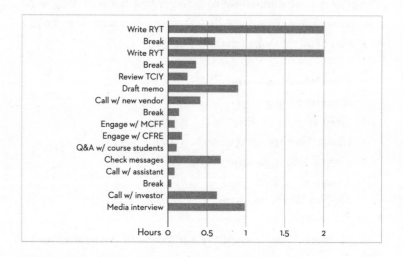

yesterday, which illustrates the contrast between deep and shallow work throughout my day.

Because I am so productive in the first half of my day, I am completely at peace with the variable nature of the second half. By lunchtime, I've already gotten my most important work done. Plus, knowing that I don't have very much willpower left over anyway, I'm fine spending much of my time in the shallows.

The second half of my day is also where I confine opportunities for serendipity. When I was running the daily operations of Threshold 360, this was the time in which I would have more of an open-door policy. In the mornings, I was holed away with my headphones on and the door closed. In the afternoons, it was much more likely that my headphones would be off and the door would be open for anyone to enter.

If you've made it this far in the chapter and you're still not fully sold on the value of depth, it's likely because you understand the significant value of seemingly random interactions throughout the day. Some of the best ideas I've ever had at work came from unscheduled brainstorming sessions in my office or casual conversations in the hallways.

Of course, these types of interactions aren't just good for creativity. They are also one of the ways God speaks to us. As much as C. S. Lewis longed for time to do deep work, he also recognized this truth, saying, "The great thing, if one can, is to stop regarding all the unpleasant things as interruptions of one's 'own,' or 'real' life. The truth is of course that what one calls the interruptions are precisely one's real life—the life God is sending one day by day."[39]

As Christians, we understand that no interruption is an accident. But remember, not even Jesus engaged every interruption and distraction. Doing the work God has called us to do requires tremendous focus. And that necessitates confining opportunities for interruptions to *specific* times on our calendars.

Am I suggesting we can confine God to specific blocks on our calendars? Of course not. If God wants to get my attention, he will find a way. But until he does, I'm going to fight to focus on the work I believe he has called me to do.*

Am I suggesting we can confine God to specific blocks on our calendars? Of course not. If God wants to get my attention, he will find a way. But until he does, I'm going to fight to focus on the work I believe he has called me to do.

COLLECTING THE PUZZLE PIECES

I'm praying that the practices from this chapter help you ward off the enemies in your fight for depth, ensuring you are much more present and productive. But to be as effective as possible in working toward God's purposes in the world, it's critical that we understand just how productive three God-designed rhythms of rest can be. That's the sixth piece of the puzzle for redeeming your time that we'll pick up in the next chapter.

---

*The practices in this chapter have shown you how to make time for depth in your daily schedule. If you're interested in going deeper (See what I did there?) on this topic, check out this chapter's corresponding videos at JordanRaynor.com/RYT. In those videos, I'll show you two practices for cultivating depth on a one-off basis at work and home: the "grand gesture" and "mega-batching."

CHAPTER 6

EMBRACE PRODUCTIVE REST

To redeem our time in the model of our Redeemer, we must embrace the God-designed rhythms of rest that are counterintuitively productive for our goals and our souls.

S hay Cochrane was frustrated. For two months in a row, Social Squares, her styled-stock photography business, had put up disappointing growth numbers. Although Cochrane's team and product line had matured over the years, it was clear that the company's marketing strategies had not. As Cochrane explained, "We were still utilizing the same shoestring marketing strategies that had been put in place years before. It was really no surprise that they were no longer working."[1]

The problems rolling around Cochrane's head were endless. "I knew we needed to drive more traffic to our new website," she recalled. "We needed better lead magnets. We needed to give people sharable content to repost. We needed to add value to the product as competition grew. The list went on and on."[2]

Cochrane could clearly see the laundry list of problems in her business. What she *couldn't* see was a unifying strategy for solving them. Her list of need-tos felt like one-off tactics rather than a comprehensive plan for growth. As Cochrane explained, "The weight of the variety of present issues was looming in my head from day to day, but I had yet to put pen to paper to devise an actual plan."[3]

Then one night, something remarkable happened. "I woke up around 3:00 a.m. with my head running a hundred miles an hour, as if I had been somehow already working on the solution to all of these problems while I slept," Cochrane said. "I lay there for a few minutes, chalking it up to just anxiously fussing over issues instead of trusting God that it could wait until tomorrow. But I quickly realized that what was coming together in my head was a very detailed and well-developed strategy that would solve 90 percent of the issues that had been dogging our business the past two months."⁴

Cochrane couldn't believe what was happening. Without even trying, all her problems were being solved *in her sleep.* She said, "I grappled around in my nightstand drawer for my journal while trying not to wake my husband and quietly slipped out our bedroom door into the quiet dark of the living room. I clicked on the light and sat poised on the edge of the couch, journal open and pen in hand, furiously writing. Thoughts were coming so quickly and in such precise order that all I could do was try to take notes quickly enough to keep up. Thirty minutes and three pages later, I had the complete framework of what would become the simple strategy to solve nearly all the problems facing our business."⁵

With her plan written down, Cochrane slipped back into bed and fell right back to sleep. When her team executed the strategy the next month, the company's growth rate increased 700 percent.

For months before that night, dozens of seemingly disconnected problems and ideas were piling up in Cochrane's mind. But the solution didn't appear while she was straining in front of her laptop. It took a good night's sleep for her brain to connect the problems together and for a creative, unifying solution to emerge.

Cochrane's story might sound like a miracle—an anomaly that you can only pray will happen to you. But as we'll see in this chapter, nothing could be further from the truth. Our stories may not be as dramatic as Cochrane's, but each of us has the potential to experience what she experienced that night: the biblically based, scientifically verified truth that rest is a counterintuitive key to being wildly productive.

In our "hustle" culture, this truth is easily overlooked. The world will often tell you that if you want to get more done, you must "work harder," "burn the midnight oil," or "sleep when you're dead." In this chapter, I'll propose that the *opposite* is true. In order to do more, most of us need to *do less* and *rest more*.

In order to do more, most of us need to do less and rest more.

And I'm not just talking about sleep. Scientists have discovered that there are bi-hourly, nightly, and weekly rhythms of productive rest embedded in our God-designed DNA. Ignoring these rhythms leads to burnout, anxiety, and unproductiveness as we seek to do our most exceptional work for the glory of God and the good of others. In this chapter, I'll first build a case for each of these three productive rhythms of rest. Then I'll recommend three practices for integrating these rhythms into your life.

THREE RHYTHMS OF PRODUCTIVE REST

Rhythm #1: Bi-Hourly Breaks

When I first discovered the principle of deep work, I was hooked. Because my blocks of undistracted work enabled me to be so much more productive, I wanted to get as much deep work done as I could, so I'd sit at my laptop from early morning to late afternoon, only getting up for lunch or a bathroom break. In the arrogance of my more youthful self, I ignored the science that shows you can do only about four hours of hyperfocused work in a day. I also failed to recognize that my brain, eyes, and soul were *screaming* for a break. I was treating my days as sprints: going as hard and fast as I could until I finally collapsed in the afternoon. But over time, I learned through experience and study that this is just not how God designed us to run. God created us to operate not as if we're in a sprint or a marathon but as if we're doing a *workout*.

In chapter 5, we saw that focus is akin to a physical muscle we would work out at the gym. As anyone who works out knows, the only way to make a physical workout sustainable is to rest in between reps. Just as our physical muscles need rest to finish a workout, our focus muscles need rest to finish the work the Father has given us to do.

Few people have studied this topic more deeply than Tony Schwartz, CEO of the Energy Project. Schwartz said,

> Human beings are not designed to run like computers—at high speeds, continuously, for long periods of time. . . .
> *We're designed to pulse.* (emphasis added)[6]

Designed is a terrific choice of word because, as scientists have discovered, God has hardwired us to pulse every other hour in what are called ultradian cycles. Essentially, our brains move from higher to lower levels of alertness every ninety minutes. At the end of that ninety-minute cycle, our brains need a break. Ultradian cycles are the body's way of demanding that we work for ninety minutes, rest for fifteen to thirty, and start all over again, repeating the cycle on a bi-hourly basis throughout the day.

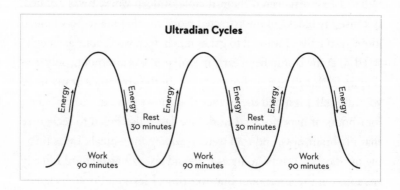

When I first read about ultradian cycles, I had a hard time accepting this phenomenon to be true, even though the data is indisputable. I'm a hardworking guy, so the idea of taking significant breaks every two hours sounded *crazy* to me. But after ending enough days feeling exhausted and burned out, I began to accept that maybe I *did* have a God-designed internal clock that was pushing me to rest, so I decided to give these bi-hourly breaks a try. Every ninety minutes, I'd get up from my desk for fifteen to thirty minutes to go on a walk or call my wife. If I was at home, I'd do the dishes or fold laundry. At first these breaks felt like a colossal waste of time, but it didn't take long for me to realize that they were counterintuitively one of the most productive additions to my day. Why? Because when done right, bi-hourly breaks almost completely restore my energy. Ironically, these brief rests help me get more *and* better work done.

Of course, I'm far from the only person to experience this. Leonardo da Vinci was attuned to this rhythm of rest more than five hundred years ago, taking frequent breaks in between sprints of painting. "To remain constantly at work will diminish your judgment," da Vinci said. "Go some distance away, because work will be in perspective and a lack of harmony is more readily seen."[7]

To cite a couple of modern examples, 90 percent of more than 2,000 employees at Sony reported increased performance after taking breaks throughout their workdays.[8] This same discovery was made by the violinists in the study that led to the 10,000-Hour Rule. As we saw in the previous chapter, the top-performing violinists in that famed study shared two things in common: they *worked* harder in ninety-minute blocks of deep work, and they *rested* harder, taking breaks in between each block of practice. Oh yeah, and they also got nearly an hour more of sleep than their less masterful counterparts, which brings us to our second rhythm of productive rest.[9]

Rhythm #2: Nightly Sleep

According to the National Sleep Foundation, more than half of American adults fail to obtain the recommended seven to nine hours of sleep each weeknight.[10] Who cares? The World Health Organization, for starters, who now labels our collective lack of sleep an "emerging global epidemic."[11]

Dr. Matthew Walker—a professor of neuroscience and psychology at the University of California, Berkeley, and one of the world's most renowned experts on sleep—explained why this is such a critical issue. In his bestselling book *Why We Sleep*, Walker summarized research linking sleep to our productivity, saying that a failure to get adequate sleep is worse for your performance than "an equivalent absence of food or exercise" or *showing up to work drunk*.[12]

But it's not just our performance that suffers when we fail to catch our zzzs. A lack of sleep is also detrimental to our health. Summarizing the data, Walker said, "Routinely sleeping less than six or seven hours a night demolishes your immune system, substantially increasing your risk of certain forms of cancer . . . [and] contributes to all major psychiatric conditions, including depression, anxiety, and suicidality."[13] In other words, the less time you sleep, the less time you have to do good works for the glory of God and the good of others.

The less time you sleep, the less time you have to do good works for the glory of God and the good of others.

But what I find more motivating than the scary side effects of a lack of sleep are the tremendous benefits of a good night's sleep. Here are just four:

First, as you've likely experienced, adequate sleep helps you *concentrate* when you are trying to achieve depth at work or home.[14]

Second, sleep helps you *perfect skills* you've learned throughout the day. As one researcher explained, "When you are awake you learn new things, but when you are asleep you refine them."[15] It turns out that "practice does not make perfect. It is practice, followed by a night of sleep, that leads to perfection."[16]

Third, adequate sleep has been linked to the ability to *earn more income*. According to a study conducted by economists Matthew

Gibson and Jeffrey Shrader, "A one-hour increase in long-run average sleep increases wages by 16%."[17]

And the fourth and, in my opinion, most fascinating benefit is that sleep *enhances creative problem solving*. This is precisely what we saw in the case of Shay Cochrane. But Cochrane is far from the only person to experience massive creative breakthroughs after a solid stretch of sleep. A twenty-two-year-old Larry Page conceived of Google in a dream in which he "had somehow managed to download the entire Web and just keep the links."[18] Paul McCartney wrote two of the Beatles' most famous songs—"Let It Be" and "Yesterday"—in his sleep,[19] as did filmmaker James Cameron with *The Terminator* and *Avatar*.[20] But my favorite story of sleep-enhancing, creative problem solving came from the inventor Thomas Edison:

> Edison would nap sitting up in a chair, with his arms draped over the sides and a steel ball in each hand. On the floor on either side of the chair was a metal pan. If he fell too deeply asleep, the balls would fall with a clatter, awakening him in time for him to rescue any useful thought before it flashed back into the cognitive vapor.[21]

Those are fun stories, but is there any science to back up this idea that sleep enhances creative problem solving? There is—loads of it. In one study, a sleep researcher named Dr. Ullrich Wagner asked the participants to work on hundreds of difficult math problems for more than an hour at a time.[22] At the start of the experiment, participants were provided with specific rules for working through the problems. What they *weren't* told was that researchers had embedded a "hidden rule, or shortcut, common across all the problems."[23] Participants who discovered this shortcut would be able to solve significantly more problems in much less time, but they would have to make creative connections to find the hack.

After working the problems, participants were given a twelve-hour break. Some were told to spend those twelve hours staying awake throughout the day, while others were asked to get a full eight hours of sleep. After the twelve-hour break, all participants returned for a second round of solving the numeric problems.

After the second test, the researchers asked participants if they had found the hidden shortcut. Of the participants who stayed awake, only one-fifth found the shortcut. Conversely, of the participants who got a full night's sleep, "almost 60% returned and had the 'ah-ha!' moment of spotting the hidden cheat—which is a threefold difference in creative solution insight afforded by sleep!"[24]

Incredible. "Sleep provides a nighttime theater in which your brain tests out and builds connections between vast stores of information," Dr. Walker explained.[25] "It is the difference between knowledge (retention of individual facts) and wisdom (knowing what they all mean when you fit them together)."[26] With that in mind, it makes perfect sense "that you have never been told to 'stay awake on a problem.' Instead, you are instructed to 'sleep on it.'"[27]

We create value for others (and ourselves) when we use our God-given creativity to solve problems that are far from obvious. For this benefit alone, sleeping is one of the most productive things we can do as we seek to redeem our time. Just as Dr. Martin Luther King Jr. argued that we have a moral obligation to make time for silent reflection, D. A. Carson, the theologian and cofounder of the Gospel Coalition, used the same strong words in reference to sleep. "You are morally obligated to try to get the sleep you need," Carson said. "Sometimes the godliest thing you can do in the universe is get a good night's sleep—not pray all night, but sleep."[28]

Why such strong language from Carson? Because he understands that, much like bi-hourly breaks, nightly sleep makes us more productive as we work on behalf of God's agenda in the world.

I know that getting seven or eight hours of sleep every night can sound impossible. (Remember, I have three kids ages six and under.) But as I'll show in the practices in this chapter, this moral obligation is absolutely attainable. If I can do it, you can too. But before we look at practical tips for baking bi-hourly breaks and nightly sleep into our schedules, we need to build a case for our third and final productive rhythm of rest: Sabbath.

Rhythm #3: Weekly Sabbath

In the mid-1800s, Americans fled to the west in droves in search of gold and a better life. But according to *The Emigrants' Guide to California*, published in 1849, it was the gold rushers who rested *most* (specifically by observing the Sabbath) that paradoxically reached their destination the most quickly. The guide advised, "If you rest one day out of seven you will get to California *20 days sooner* than others who don't" (emphasis added).[29]

Of course, gold rushers aren't the only people who have found Sabbath rest to be counterintuitively productive. There's plenty of evidence for this today. Chick-fil-A is likely the most well-known example in the world of business. In the early days, the restaurant chain's commitment to observing the Sabbath by staying closed on Sundays *infuriated* landlords at malls, where nearly all Chick-fil-As were located at the time. But eventually "what the mall landlords learned is that Chick-fil-A produced as many sales in six days as the other food tenants did in seven. In almost every case, Chick-fil-A had the highest volume of sales out of all the food tenants in the mall," making them one of the most highly sought-after tenants today.[30]

But Sabbath doesn't just help us do more with the time we have. There is increasing evidence that regular Sabbath observance may *extend our lives*. Dan Buettner, a *National Geographic* Fellow who has spent years trying to "reverse engineer longevity," found that Seventh-Day Adventists—who follow strict guidelines about food, exercise, and, as their name suggests, Sabbath—live an average of *ten years longer* than the average American.[31] Commenting on this phenomenon, Dr. Wayne Dysinger said, "The data is clear, the data has been published, the data has been peer reviewed. There's really not a lot of argument that people [living] this lifestyle, live longer."[32]

John Mark Comer "did the math: If [you] Sabbath every seven days, it adds up to—wait for it—*ten years* over a lifetime. Almost exactly. So when [we] say the Sabbath is life giving, that's not empty rhetoric . . . every day you Sabbath, you're (statistically and scientifically) likely to get back an elongated life."[33] Talk about redeeming one's time! By trading in one day a week, I might get *ten more years* to chase hard after the work I believe God has created me to do? Sign me up.

Hang on, Jordan, I'm no mathematician, but if you give up *ten years to gain* ten years, isn't it all a wash? Not at all, because those ten years of resting one day out of seven makes you much more productive the other six days of the week.

So, if Sabbath—this weekly rhythm of rest—is so productive, why don't we all do it? Because most of us view Sabbath as a boring, legalistic, life-sucking chore, *if* we think of it at all.

Growing up, I hardly ever thought about Sabbath, even though I grew up in the church. Nobody my family knew treated Sunday any different than any other day of the week. Sure, I'd hear about the fourth commandment from time to time, but it was one of those rules everyone seemed comfortable ignoring—kind of like the speed limit. In the rare moments that I *did* think about Sabbath, it looked like a day filled with things I *couldn't* do rather than a day filled with joyful things I *could* do.

But then about four years ago, in the middle of a particularly crazy season of life, I reread what Jesus himself said about Sabbath, and it totally changed my perspective. It seemed as though two thousand years ago, Jesus was agreeing that Sabbath had become a legalistic chore. Check out Mark 3:1–4:

Jesus went into the synagogue, and a man with a shriveled hand was there. Some of them were looking for a reason to accuse

Jesus, so they watched him closely to see if he would heal him on the Sabbath. Jesus said to the man with the shriveled hand, "Stand up in front of everyone."

Then Jesus asked them, "Which is lawful on the Sabbath: to do good or to do evil, to save life or to kill?" But they remained silent.

Talk about life-sucking legalism—literally. Here the Pharisees were criticizing Jesus for doing something life giving because it didn't adhere to the letter of the law of Sabbath. But notice that Jesus didn't say the law was irrelevant. Rather, he said the Pharisees were completely missing the point. In the passage that immediately precedes this one, Jesus said, "The Sabbath was made *for man*, not man for the Sabbath" (2:27). What did Jesus mean by that? To answer that question, let's examine a quick history of Sabbath.

The first Sabbath day was the seventh day of creation. Genesis 2:2–3 says, "By the seventh day God had finished the work he had been doing; so on the seventh day he rested from all his work. Then God blessed the seventh day and made it holy, because on it he rested from all the work of creating that he had done." It's interesting to note that Sabbath is the first "holy" object in history. On the previous six days, God saw everything that he had made and deemed it "good" or "very good," but Sabbath was the first thing God called "holy." As one writer has noted, "In a world where Wi-Fi boosters are attached to church steeples, no place remains sacred."[34] But although no *place* may remain sacred, Sabbath remains a sacred "sanctuary in time."[35]

Okay, so God rested, thus creating the first Sabbath day. But it's not until Mount Sinai that God commanded the Israelites to imitate his rhythm of working for six days and resting one:

Remember the Sabbath day by keeping it holy. Six days you shall labor and do all your work, but the seventh day is a sabbath to the Lord your God. On it you shall not do any work, neither you, nor your son or daughter, nor your male or female servant, nor your animals, nor any foreigner residing in your towns. For in six days the LORD made the heavens and the earth, the sea, and all that is in them, but he rested on the seventh day. Therefore the LORD blessed the Sabbath day and made it holy. (Exodus 20:8–11)

All right, so Sabbath is about mimicking God's rhythm of work and rest, taking a break to simply enjoy him and the good things he's given us through our work. But it's also about something else. Consider the context of when the Ten Commandments were handed down to Moses. These commandments were given just weeks after Israel's exodus from Egypt, where they had been in slavery for more than four hundred years. That's more than *four centuries'* worth of backbreaking work under the hands of ruthless slave masters screaming, "Get back to your work!" (5:4), and, "Make the work harder" (5:9). So yes, Sabbath is about stepping back and saying of our work and lives that this is "very good," but it is also about saying no to the tyranny of more. It's about declaring our freedom from slavery. It's an invitation to "stop" (the literal meaning of the Hebrew word *Shabbat*). Stop working, stop striving, stop hustling. Just stop. Sounds pretty life giving in the midst of our modern-day "hustle" culture, am I right?

Okay, so God rests and commands the Israelites to do the same. Now is when we get into trouble. Over time, God's people take the good gift of Sabbath and regulate it more than the federal government, adding *more than 1,500 rules* of what a person could and could not do on God's holy day.[36] With the addition of all these man-made rules and regulations, Sabbath, which God created to be life giving, had become life draining.

So, that's the historical backdrop of the exchange we read a few minutes ago between Jesus and the Pharisees. When Jesus said that Sabbath is "for man," he was reminding us that Sabbath is not about keeping hundreds of rules. Sabbath is about enjoying God and his good gifts and declaring that we are no longer slaves to sin, Egypt, employers, clients, marketers, email, smartphones, or the constant demands for more. We are *free*.

> *Sabbath is about enjoying God and his good gifts and declaring that we are no longer slaves to sin, Egypt, employers, clients, marketers, email, smartphones, or the constant demands for more. We are free.*

In just a minute, we'll explore what it looks like practically to open and enjoy the good gift of Sabbath, but for now I'll just say this: Sabbath is *the most life-giving thing* my family does each week—by far. Sabbath isn't another thing I "have" to do on my to-do list. Sabbath is "an island of get-to in a sea of have-to."[37]

Have you ever watched someone conducting a choir? As the singers stand silently, the conductor moves her hands down, in, out, and finally up. It's on the upswing that the singers take their breath. *That* is a picture of Sabbath. Sabbath is the upswing of my family's week, allowing us to catch our breath, energizing us for the week ahead.

REST IS PRODUCTIVE FOR OUR GOALS AND OUR SOULS

Throughout the Gospels, we see Jesus embodying the three rhythms of productive rest we've discussed in this chapter. He offered restorative breaks to his disciples as they worked (see Mark 6:30–32), he fought for sleep (see 4:38–39), and, as we've already seen, he reaffirmed the goodness of Sabbath (see 2:27).

Of course, because he is our creator, Jesus knew these rhythms of rest would help us get more done for his glory and the good of others. In other words, Jesus recognized what centuries of scientific exploration have now empirically proven: that rest is productive as we strive toward our goals. But Jesus also undoubtedly knew something science may never be able to prove: rest is not just productive for our *goals;* it is also productive for our *souls*.

Taking bi-hourly breaks throughout our workdays is productive for our souls because it reminds us that God doesn't need us to finish our to-do lists. Getting a full night's sleep is productive for our souls because it reminds us that God is the only being who neither slumbers nor sleeps (see Psalm 121:4) and thus doesn't need us to keep the world spinning. Sabbath is productive for our souls because it reminds us that "all time belongs to God and stands under the renewing lordship of Jesus Christ."[38] And ultimately all these rhythms of rest are productive for our souls because they are a means of preaching the gospel to ourselves and those around us. Rest is a way of reminding ourselves that no matter how productive we are, no matter how many good works we accomplish, we are God's beloved children, in whom he is well pleased. All of this brings us to the sixth principle for redeeming our time.

PRINCIPLE #6
EMBRACE PRODUCTIVE REST

To redeem our time in the model of our Redeemer, we must embrace the God-designed rhythms of rest that are counterintuitively productive for our goals and our souls.

How do we practically incorporate these bi-hourly, nightly, and weekly rhythms of rest into our modern lives? Here are three practices.

PRACTICE 1: BREAK WELL EVERY OTHER HOUR

As mentioned previously, our God-designed ultradian cycles ensure that after ninety minutes of focused, deep work, our energy will be depleted and in need of renewal. But not just any break will be restorative. We have to learn the art of breaking well throughout our workday.

There are two ingredients to truly restorative breaks: a significant *quantity* of time and the *quality* of activities done during the break. How long should your bi-hourly breaks be? I recommend fifteen to thirty minutes, but really the quality of the break trumps its length. For me, ten minutes washing dishes is far more restorative than spending thirty minutes playing on my phone. Doing dishes might not be the thing for you, though. The best advice I can give here is to experiment with different activities to find which types of breaks most restore your energy and ability to focus.

As a general rule, though, I (and countless people I have interviewed on my podcast) can confirm the wisdom of this age-old adage: if you work with your mind, rest with your hands; if you work with your hands, rest with your mind. For example, if you're a carpenter, it won't be very restorative for you to rest by chopping wood. Conversely, if you're a programmer sitting in front of a computer all day, it probably won't be very restorative for you to rest while reading news on your laptop.

> *If you work with your mind, rest with your hands; if you work with your hands, rest with your mind.*

Winston Churchill, who worked with his mind as a phenomenally productive writer and statesman, understood the value of resting with his hands. Churchill famously created more than 550 paintings in his lifetime and loved laying bricks outside his home. He once said that an ideal day would consist of "200 bricks and 2,000 words."[39] The "work" of painting and bricklaying didn't wear Churchill down. On the contrary, this type of rest *invigorated* him. In an essay titled "Painting as a Pastime," Churchill explained why:

A man can wear out a particular part of his mind by continually using it and tiring it, just in the same way he can wear out the elbows of his coat. . . . The tired parts of the mind can be rested and strengthened not merely by rest, but by using other parts.[40]

On my podcast, former CEO of SeaWorld Joel Manby expounded the same wisdom as Churchill. Before going to SeaWorld, Manby would rest his mind by working out his hands while playing the piano. But once he arrived at SeaWorld in the middle of the public relations crisis caused by the documentary *Blackfish*, Manby's habit of productive rest began to slip. As he recalls,

At SeaWorld . . . I [stopped resting] because I was getting phone calls from my activist investor . . . at four in the morning, 5:30 in the morning.

Emails at 2 in the morning and he expected responses and I would go 20 hours a day, literally seven days a week trying to turn [SeaWorld] around and I became very unhealthy in a lot of ways. . . . It was a horrible period.[41]

His unhealthy state contributed to the demise of his marriage and compromised his ability to deal with an extremely difficult board of directors. Looking back, Manby said, "I really had a dark period because I got away from the great habits. . . . So I think those daily routines you talk about are just critical to keep us tied with what Jesus wants from us."[42]

So, which specific habits do I recommend in order for you to renew your energy throughout the day? Here are *my* three favorites: running, eating lunch with my kids, and washing dishes. You'll notice that I prefer bi-hourly breaks that serve as double wins. Each of them is productive to some end *in addition to* reenergizing me for the work I have to do the rest of the day. When I run, I exercise my body *and* restore my energy. When I eat lunch, I spend quality time with my kids *and* rest my mind. When I wash the dishes, I serve my family *and* give my brain a much needed break.

Those are the activities that help me break well. Here are some other ideas for bi-hourly breaks to restore your energy throughout the day, organized by where you work physically.

At Home

- Do the dishes.
- Fold the laundry.
- Take out the trash.
- Play an instrument.
- Doodle or paint (while channeling your inner Churchill).
- Do some yard work.
- Take a nap. (J. R. R. Tolkien and Winston Churchill were nappers.[43] Not my cup of tea, but it may be yours.)

At the Office

- "Walk the ship"[44] to connect with coworkers on a personal level (as long as they're not trying to cultivate depth).
- Play foosball (if you're working for one of *those* tech start-ups).

Anywhere

- Go for a walk or run.
- Call your spouse or a friend to chat about something other than work.
- Make a cup of coffee or tea.
- Eat lunch away from your desk.
- Build with Legos.
- Listen to a piece of music. (Bach's *Cello Suite No. 1 in G Major*, anyone? Or Taylor Swift, obviously.)

- Read a book. (Probably not best if you work with your mind!)
- Do a crossword puzzle. (Again, best for those who work with their hands.)

Choose one or two of the ideas above to experiment with this week and experience the energizing impact of breaking well.

PRACTICE 2: CREATE AN EIGHT-HOUR SLEEP OPPORTUNITY EVERY NIGHT

I can already hear your objection. *Jordan, I don't need eight hours of sleep. I'm good on five or six hours.* I won't call you a liar, but science will. Again, here's world-renowned sleep expert Dr. Matthew Walker: "Sixty years of scientific research prevent me from accepting anyone who tells me that he or she can 'get by on just four or five hours of sleep a night just fine.'"[45]

Okay, Jordan, but surely seven *hours of sleep is fine, right?* I thought so too. In fact, for many years, I operated on seven hours of sleep. But it turns out that won't cut it. According to the data, "After ten days of just seven hours of sleep, the brain is as dysfunctional as it would be after going without sleep for twenty-four hours."[46] Yikes. Apologies to everyone I served during years of operating on only seven hours of sleep.

But, Jordan, I feel fine *on less than eight hours, so who cares?* Here comes the scariest part: research has proven over and over again that we are *terrible* at estimating how much sleep we get and the impact a lack of sleep has on our performance. One study in the *American Journal of Epidemiology* found that most people get 20 percent less sleep than they think they do.[47] So, if you think you're getting seven hours of sleep, the data says you're likely getting only about five and a half!

Not only are we awful at estimating *how much* sleep we get, but we also have serious trouble recognizing the *impact* our lack of sleep has on our performance. Summarizing the results of one study, researchers at the University of Pennsylvania said this:

> After a week or two of sleep restriction, subjects were markedly impaired and less alert, but rated themselves subjectively as only moderately sleepy. . . . This suggests that people frequently underestimate the cognitive impact of sleep restriction and overestimate their performance readiness when sleep restricted.[48]

This is the equivalent of having too much to drink and confidently saying you're okay to drive. Just as friends don't let friends drive drunk, friends don't let friends get inadequate sleep if they care about redeeming their time. Are there exceptions to the eight-hour sleep rule? Yes. There's a genetic mutation that enables some people to thrive on less sleep. But before you think you're one of those people, consider this: according to researchers, "This mutation is exceedingly rare, occurring in fewer than one in 4 million people."[49] You're six times more likely to win an Olympic gold medal (odds: 1 in 662,000)[50] than to have this rare gene. For the vast majority of us, there's simply no way around this inescapable fact: loving your neighbor as yourself starts with getting eight hours of sleep.

Loving your neighbor as yourself starts with getting eight hours of sleep.

We may not like this fact, but it doesn't make it any less true. Trust me, I *hate* what science has proven on this topic, because I know how hard it is to get this much sleep! As mentioned, my wife and I have three kids ages six and under, one of whom just turned a year old. If you've ever had young children, you know that *I am in the fight of my life* for adequate sleep. But by the grace of God and a not insignificant amount of sacrifice, Kara and I *both* get seven and a half to eight hours of sleep nearly every night. How? Here's the five-point checklist we use.

#1: Set a Bedtime

Almost everyone I know has a set time that they wake up each morning, but very few have a time that they routinely go to bed. They say something like, "I go to bed sometime between nine and eleven, depending on what I'm watching on TV." Apologies if you share a similar perspective on when you go to bed, but this is *insane* to me. It's simple math. If your wake-up time is fixed (and for most of us it is), it is impossible to consistently get eight hours of sleep if you don't consistently go to bed at least eight hours before your alarm goes off. Rocket science, I know.

While I was writing this chapter, a friend sent me the *Wall Street Journal*'s "guide to superior slumber,"[51] which listed dozens of products you could buy to enhance your sleep, including a $27 pair of socks,[52] $140 botanical wallpaper,[53] and a $1,040 Louis Vuitton mink sleep mask.[54] I'm not making this up. You know what's *free* and will have a *far greater impact* on your ability to get adequate sleep? Setting a bedtime.

Keep in mind, however, that time in bed does not equal time asleep. We have to account for what sleep scientists call "sleep efficiency," which is the percentage of time you actually sleep while in bed.[55] The older you get, the less efficient your sleep becomes. Healthy teenagers enjoy a sleep efficiency of roughly 95 percent, meaning that if they're in bed for eight hours, they're actually getting a little more than seven and a half hours of sleep.[56] By the time you hit your sixties, sleep efficiency falls to just over 80 percent. The rest of us fall somewhere in the middle.[57]

Of course, what this means is that if you really want to fight for eight hours of *sleep*, doctors will tell you to create a nightly "adequate sleep opportunity time" of "at least eight or nine hours in bed."[58] I don't know about you, but *nine* hours in bed is where I draw the line. There's simply *no way* I can pull that off every day and pursue excellence in all things at home and work. That's why I give myself a sleep opportunity of slightly more than eight hours. Nearly every night, I lay my head on my pillow between 8:45 and 8:55 and wake up consistently at five in the morning. According to my Fitbit data, I log close to eight hours of *actual* sleep each night. Thank you, Lord, for good sleep-efficient genes!

#2: Stop Striving at Least an Hour Before Bed

After my kids go to bed at seven, my wife and I spend a few minutes doing some productive things at home.* We pick up the house, make the kids' lunches for the next day, take out the trash, and so on. Our goal is to be done with all productive things by seven thirty. That's when we force ourselves to begin winding down. As I shared in chapter 3, that is when we put our phones to bed and just enjoy each other's company. We sit, talk, read, and watch TV. I know many productivity gurus who are adamant about "no screens before bed." That's just not my style. Ending our day with *The Crown, Parks and Recreation,* or *The West Wing* works for Kara and me. We go to bed *just* fine. Whatever works for you works.

#3: Avoid Caffeine and Alcohol in the Late Afternoon and Evenings

Avoiding caffeine is obvious, but many people believe that alcohol helps them sleep. It's true that alcohol helps you *fall* asleep, but that

---

*Yes, I recognize that I have the privilege of having young kids who go to bed at seven. How am I going to make this all work when they're teenagers? I have no idea. Check back with me in ten years.

sleep is almost always *extremely* fragmented. I've got the Fitbit data to prove it. According to doctors at Sleep Foundation, "Alcohol is a sedative" that "decreases overall sleep quality [and] can result in shorter sleep duration and more sleep disruptions."[59]

#4: Make Your Bedroom as Dark as Possible

Light interrupts sleep, so invest in good curtains, unplug your nightlights, and put your phone in another room while you rest (or, at a minimum, keep it facedown on your nightstand). Kara jokes that my commitment to good sleep is going to lead to my buying that thousand-dollar Louis Vuitton sleep mask. I haven't gone as far as a sleep mask yet, but if I do, the brand will be Amazon Essentials.

#5: Make Your Bedroom as Cold as Possible

Sleep scientists recommend 65 degrees Fahrenheit, which sounds *crazy* to me. But yeah, it should be cool. Nobody sleeps well in sweltering heat.

As with all of the practices in this book, strict legalism with this five-point sleep checklist isn't helpful. Yes, there are nights in which I don't go to bed right at eight forty-five, and just last night I had a beer with some friends right before I hit the sack. But these exceptions are becoming rarer and rarer as I experience just how productive sleeping well can be as I seek to redeem my time and serve others through the ministry of excellence each day.

PRACTICE 3: CEASE AND FEAST ONCE A WEEK

My kids have virtually no concept of time. Almost every morning, my two eldest daughters, Ellison and Kate, rush out of their rooms and ask, "Daddy, is it Sabbath Sunday?" All week long, the five of us eagerly look forward to our family's day of rest. So, what does Sabbath look like in the Raynor household? How do we accept God's coun-terintuitively productive gift of rest?

Ironically, it starts with work. Hebrews 4:10–11 says, "Anyone who enters God's rest also rests from their works, just as God did from his. Let us, therefore, make every effort to enter that rest." Whether it's taking breaks throughout the day, fighting for eight hours of sleep, or enjoying the gift of Sabbath, we have to make an effort to rest well.

Our family observes the Sabbath on Sunday, so we begin preparing for Sabbath on Saturday afternoon. Our goal is to knock out every-thing we need to get done in order to focus solely on . . . well . . . rest. Here are the recurring to-dos on our Sabbath preparation checklist (of course logged in my Commitment Tracking System):

- *Make a plan for Sabbath Sunday:* On Saturday, we decide what we're going to eat and do and who, if anyone, we will see on Sunday. If we are going to hang out with family or friends, we try to coordinate when and where we will meet them, before Sabbath begins. This helps us avoid spending all day Sunday tethered to our phones, texting back and forth to make plans.
- *Pack for church:* This saves *a lot* of stress and hurry on Sunday mornings. On Saturday, we pack the car with everything we will need for church the next day (waters for the kids, tithe check, and so on).
- *Pick up the house:* We don't do a deep clean of our house, but we do make sure that everything within sight belongs "where it is, the way it is." Removing visual distractions helps us focus on God's Word and each other on Sabbath.
- *Do the laundry:* We batch all our laundry on Saturdays rather than doing it throughout the week.* The goal is to have every-thing washed, dried, and put away before Sabbath begins.

---

*For more on why and how this saves us time, check out the free video on mega-batching at JordanRaynor.com/RYT.

- *Run the dishwasher:* Sabbath starts with no dishes in the sink pulling at our attention.
- *Send my phone on a twenty-four-hour vacation:* Once all of the above is done, I turn my phone on Airplane Mode and keep it that way until Sunday evening. Kara has chosen a more moderate approach, keeping her phone on but for the most part keeping it out of sight and out of mind for twenty-four hours.

Executing that short checklist takes a couple of hours each Saturday. Once the last item is checked off, our work is done and all striving ceases in our home. If we forgot to fold a load of laundry, it will have to wait until Monday. If there's a dish left in the sink, we leave it be.

And it's not just physical work we steer clear of. We also try our best to set aside productive conversations for twenty-four hours. Again, Sabbath is about enjoying what God's *already* given us, not worrying about or longing for what he might give us tomorrow. If you were in our home during Sabbath, you'd likely hear Kara and me talking about things we're grateful for God doing through our work the past week, but we try our hardest not to talk about problems we have to solve in the week ahead or who is going to drive who where on Tuesday night.

Okay, so those are the things we stop doing on Sabbath. But this rhythm of rest isn't just about what we *don't* do. It's also about the life-giving things we *do* do. Sabbath is a day for ceasing *and* feasting.

I want you to imagine a huge banquet hall with a beautiful table filled with the most delectable foods you can imagine. Seated at the head of the table is Jesus, and all week long, you and I are the servers, hustling and bustling to serve Jesus and his guests. Sabbath is first an invitation to cease from that work—to put down the food tray, take off your apron, and catch your breath. But here's where the analogy breaks down. In a restaurant, the servers take their breaks in the kitchen or parking lot of the restaurant. They are invited to cease, but they're never invited to feast at the tables of their guests. But you and

I are "co-heirs with Christ" (Romans 8:17). We are adopted children of God (see Ephesians 1:5). We aren't invited to just cease from our work—we are invited to pull up a chair next to King Jesus and feast on his goodness and his gifts. That's what Sabbath is: an opportunity to cease and feast, spiritually, physically, and relationally.

> *Sabbath is a day for ceasing and feasting. We aren't invited to just cease from our work—we are invited to pull up a chair next to King Jesus and feast on his goodness and his gifts.*

Here's what that looks like in our family. Once we've prepared for Sabbath and ceased doing all productive things, we light a candle to visually mark our transition into a time of rest. This ensures that, in the words of my kids, it "smells like Sabbath" (and pumpkin pecan waffles) for twenty-four glorious hours. Once the candle is lit, we feast on takeout from one of our favorite restaurants, followed by some sort of epic dessert.

On Sunday morning, I wake up at my normal time to be in the Word and in prayer. Once the kids are up, I allow them to indulge in two Sabbath-only treats: a hot cup of coffee and a full-length movie. (As I was writing this, Ellison wrote her first "opinion paper" for first grade, outlining why Sunday is the best day of the week. Unsurprisingly, coffee and a movie were reasons #1 and #2 in her argument.) Kara feasts on sleep while I watch *Tangled* with the big kids for the eightieth time.

After that, we usually head to our favorite doughnut shop in town. On the short drive, we hold one of my favorite traditions: sharing what we're most thankful for from the past week. With doughnuts and Cuban breakfast sandwiches in hand, we head back home with plenty of time to get ready for church, where we feast on the Word with our church family.

After church, Sabbath afternoons are usually pretty low-key:

lunch, naps, getting lost in a great book. After nap time, we may go to the beach or a park, or Kara and I might go on a date. But many Sundays, we're just hanging around the house, playing games, swimming in the pool, or running around the backyard. As my friend Jeff Heck said, sometimes Sabbath is as simple as "a kiddie pool and a beer." After dinner on Sunday, we blow out the candle, pack lunches for school, and get ready for Monday, our souls filled and ready for the week ahead.

That's how we Sabbath. What could Sabbath look like for you? What would it look like for you to cease and feast on the Lord, his Word, and the good gifts he has given you and your family this week? I'd encourage you to spend some time really thinking through that question. But please remember that, at the end of the day, Sabbath isn't about what you eat, where you go, or whether or not you let your toddlers drink a latte. It's a holy, sacred day to focus on the fact that *Jesus* is our ultimate Sabbath. As he said in Matthew 11:28, "*I* will give you rest." Whether it's taking bi-hourly breaks, getting the sleep we need each night, or accepting the gift of Sabbath each week, we can rest because Jesus's work on the cross assures us of his love *regardless* of anything we do or don't do. No matter how productive we are in a given day or week, we can embrace each of these rhythms of productive rest because we are confident of God's "never stopping, never giving up, unbreaking, always and forever love."[60]

COLLECTING THE PUZZLE PIECES

With the rhythms of productive rest you learned in this chapter, you have collected the sixth piece of the puzzle to redeeming your time. There's just one final piece we need, and it's the one that will allow us to connect the whole puzzle together in a way that ensures we model Jesus's remarkable lack of hurry.

CHAPTER 7

ELIMINATE ALL HURRY

To redeem our time in the model of our Redeemer, we must embrace productive busyness while ruthlessly eliminating hurry from our lives.

F red Rogers lived a wildly productive life. Over the course of _Mister Rogers' Neighborhood_'s thirty-one seasons, Rogers personally wrote nine hundred scripts, two hundred songs, and thirteen operas.[1] Oh yeah, and he also starred in the program, produced it, directed it, performed the music, and animated the show's puppets. Outside the studio, Rogers somehow found time to write books, make speeches, travel, and raise a healthy family.

In other words, Rogers was _busy._ And yet he was remarkably _unhurried._ As his biographer Maxwell King once explained to me, "[Rogers] did all this stuff and yet, everybody who ran into him reported the same thing, which is when they got in Fred's presence, _everything slowed down_" (emphasis added).[2] So common was this experience that Rogers' staff had a name for it: they called it "Fred-time."[3] King said that "whenever one sat down to talk with [Rogers], urgency seemed to dissipate, [and] discussion proceeded at a measured, almost otherworldly pace."[4]

That "otherworldly pace" became a hallmark of _Mister Rogers' Neighborhood._ At the beginning of each episode, the first thing viewers saw inside Mister Rogers' home wasn't the show's host but rather a blinking yellow traffic light—a not-so-subtle cue that it was time to slow down and stop hurrying. Of course, this theme was carried throughout the entire show. "Whether Fred Rogers was speaking on camera, playing in the Neighborhood of Make-Believe with King

Friday the Puppet, or singing one of his trademark songs, just about every frame of the show seemed to say: *Slow down.*"[5]

Rogers' devout Christian faith has been well documented by biographers and his former staff. One former *Neighborhood* staffer (and later vice president of the Pittsburgh Theological Seminary) said of Rogers, "I truly believe he was one of the most authentic and Christlike people that I have ever known in my life."[6] If you were to make a list of Rogers' Christlike qualities, it would certainly include his care for children, his love of outcasts, and his gentle spirit. But as we'll see in this chapter, that list should also include "Fred-time"—Rogers' remarkable ability to be crazy productive *without* being hurried. Not only was this a hallmark of Fred Rogers' life, but it is also central to the picture the Gospels paint of our Savior.

BUSY, UNHURRIED JESUS

One of the most common words used in the gospel of Mark is *immediately*. Mark employs this word "no less than forty times"[7] to make an inescapable point: the lives of Jesus and his disciples were *busy*.

One time, the disciples tried to convince Jesus to call it a day, and he replied, "Are there not twelve hours in the day?" (John 11:9, ESV). The *Cambridge Bible* commentary translates Jesus's words as follows: "Are there not twelve working-hours in which a man may labour without fear of stumbling? I have not yet reached the end of My working-day, and so can safely continue the work I came to do. The night cometh, when I can no longer work; but it has not yet come."[8] When that night *did* come, Jesus prayed to the Father, saying, "I have brought you glory on earth by finishing the work you gave me to do" (17:4). Jesus was highly motivated to finish his work as a means of glorifying the Father, and that led him to be wildly productive and busy.

But while Jesus was certainly busy, the Gospels never show him hurried. As pastor Kevin DeYoung said, "He was busy, but never in a way that made him frantic, anxious, irritable, proud, envious, or distracted by lesser things."⁹ What's the difference between busyness and hurry? I love author John Ortberg's answer to that question:

> There is a world of difference between being busy and being hurried. Being busy is an outward condition, a condition of the body. It occurs when we have many things to do. Busy-ness is inevitable in modern culture. . . . By itself, busy-ness is not lethal. Being hurried is an inner condition, a condition of the soul. It means to be so preoccupied with myself and my life that I am unable to be fully present with God, with myself, and with other people. I am unable to occupy this present moment. Busy-ness migrates to hurry when we let it squeeze God out of our lives.¹⁰

Do you see the difference? Busyness is having a lot of meetings on your calendar; hurry is scheduling those meetings back to back, forcing you to sprint from one meeting to the next without enough time to hear your own thoughts. Busyness is having a lot of errands to run; hurry is getting mad about choosing the "wrong line" at the grocery store because you have no margin for the thirty seconds you lost by choosing lane 3 instead of lane 4. Busyness is attending three Bible studies a week; hurry is not having enough time and stillness to listen to God's voice in between those studies.

Hurry is the great enemy of our ability to be purposeful, present, and productive.

Almost all of us are busy *and* hurried. And that's a problem because that is not the way of Jesus and is thus not the model for redeeming our time. Philosopher and author Dallas Willard said that "hurry is the great enemy of spiritual life in our day. You must ruthlessly eliminate hurry from your life."¹¹ As Jesus's example shows us, hurry isn't just "the great enemy of spiritual life"; hurry is also the great enemy of our ability to be purposeful, present, and productive. This truth brings us to the seventh and final principle of this book:

PRINCIPLE #7
ELIMINATE ALL HURRY

To redeem our time in the model of our Redeemer, we must embrace productive busyness while ruthlessly eliminating hurry from our lives.

To live out this principle, we need to answer this question: What is causing all our hurry in the first place? There are many answers to that question, some external and some internal. But perhaps most practically, our hurry stems from our failure to "count the cost" of our time. Jesus used this accounting terminology with his disciples in the gospel of Luke:

> Which of you, desiring to build a tower, does not first sit down and count the cost, whether he has enough to complete it? Otherwise, when he has laid a foundation and is not able to finish, all who see it begin to mock him, saying, "This man began to build and was not able to finish" (14:28–30, ESV).

Sounds like a typical Tuesday for most of us—biting off way more than we can chew in a twenty-four-hour time period. Now, to be clear, the context of this passage is that Jesus was asking his disciples to "count the cost" of following him. But, of course, Jesus's words can be wisely applied to our efforts to redeem our time. In fact, Jesus himself modeled this application in the gospel of Mark. Here's the account: "Jesus entered Jerusalem and went into the temple courts. He looked around at everything, but since it was already late, he went out to Bethany with the Twelve" (Mark 11:11). Just a few verses later, Mark tells us what Jesus had in mind originally. Here's verse 15: "On reaching Jerusalem, Jesus entered the temple courts and began driving out those who were buying and selling there. He overturned the tables of the money changers and the benches of those selling doves."

Okay, so Jesus's plan all along was to overturn some tables and drive out the vendors who were turning the temple into a "den of robbers" (verse 17). Then why not do this the night before? Why wait until the next day? Of course, we can't answer those questions definitively, but given Jesus's track record as a busy but unhurried guy, my guess is that Jesus had counted the cost of his time. Look at verse 11 again: Jesus "went into the temple courts [and] . . . looked around at everything, *but since it was already late,*" he decided not to cram any more activity into what had already been a busy day (see verses 1–10). You can almost hear him muttering to himself, "It can wait." Could Jesus have squeezed in a little table flipping before he retired for the night? Sure, but he chose not to. He had counted the cost and knew that adding anything else to his already busy day would have tipped the scales from busy to hurry.

EVERY MINUTE HAS A NAME

Dave Ramsey has helped millions of people get out of debt and experience financial freedom. How has he done it? By teaching them to count the cost of their spending via an unbelievably simple tool: a budget. A financial budget is simply a means of "[telling] *every* dollar where to go"[12] before new dollars hit your bank account. It's a way of *counting* the cost before you have an opportunity to *incur* the costs. That's why Ramsey advocates that "every dollar must have a name" in your budget.[13] It's simply good stewardship to plan where you're going to spend every dollar before those dollars are in your hands.

That's a simple concept that is widely accepted as plain old common sense today. But what boggles my mind is that although Ramsey and others have convinced millions of people to budget their money, *far fewer* of us have ever thought about budgeting our *time*. So we get to the office, open our email, and spend the rest of the day reacting rather than proactively focusing on the work we believe God has called us to do. And then we wonder how we got to the end of the day feeling as though we did nothing of value. Matt Perman said, "You are satisfied with your day when there is a match between what you value and how you spent your time."[14] But the only way to consistently achieve that level of satisfaction is to budget time for the things you value *before* you are given the time to spend.

With God's grace and provision, we can all earn more money, but none of us can earn more time. Thus, how much wiser is it to budget time rather than money? Don't get me wrong; I'm a proponent of having a financial budget, but it is time—not money—that is our most finite resource. That's why Scripture calls us to be "redeeming the *time*" and not our bank accounts, because "the *days* are evil," finite, and limited (Ephesians 5:16, NKJV). If we are to redeem our time, we would be wise to budget accordingly. We need to develop the habit of ensuring that every *minute* has a name before God gives us a fresh supply each morning.

> *We need to develop the habit of ensuring that every minute has a name before God gives us a fresh supply each morning.*

Okay, maybe not *every* minute. I'm not going to suggest you budget every second of your weekend and every bathroom break throughout the day. But even with a few exceptions, you might still object: *Name every minute? That sounds constraining, not freeing.* This is the same objection Ramsey's team has heard thousands of times about budgeting money. But as their devotees have learned, "A budget doesn't limit your freedom, it *gives* you freedom!"[15] How? By freeing you up to spend money on the things you value without constantly worrying if the next credit card swipe is going to break the bank. The same is true with budgeting your time: it frees you up to be busy without being hurried.

But, Jordan, I'm a creative. I work when inspiration strikes. I can't be confined to a schedule! That's not what more than 150 of the world's greatest artists have shown.[16] *New York Times* columnist David Brooks nailed it: "[Creative people] think like artists but work like accountants."[17]

Okay, so what does it look like practically to budget your time? The three practices in this chapter answer that question. Way back in the introduction, I told you that the seven principles in this book each represented a separate piece of the puzzle for redeeming your time. The following three practices will help you connect those pieces together. Ready? Here we go!

PRACTICE 1: BUILD A TIME BUDGET TEMPLATE

One of the keys to Fred Rogers' lack of hurry was his obsession with routine. Every night, Rogers got a full eight hours of sleep. Every day he would wake up at 5:00 a.m., read his Bible, and pray.[18] Like clockwork, by 7:00 a.m. he would be swimming his daily laps at the Pittsburgh Athletic Association.[19] So routine driven was Rogers that after his daily swim, he would weigh in at *exactly* 143 pounds *every day of his adult life.*[20] In an ode to consistency and his love of routines, Rogers' email address was zzz143@aol.com.[21]

After years of tweaking and honing his routine, Rogers had no need to hurry. He always knew what was coming next and had intentionally baked plenty of margin into his schedule. But his routine was genius in another way too: he understood that routines preserve energy throughout the day.

If you think about it, time management might be more accurately described as energy management. We can't truly manage time, but we can manage our energy *within* time. And, of course, every decision we make expends more energy.

That's what makes routines so valuable. As Greg McKeown, the author of *Essentialism,* said, "The right routines [give] us the equivalent of an energy rebate. Instead of spending our limited supply of discipline on making the same decisions again and again, embedding our decisions into our routine allows us to channel that discipline toward some other essential activity."[22]

That is why Apple cofounder Steve Jobs wore the same thing every day.[23] It's why President George W. Bush ate lunch every day at noon.[24] It's why I eat the same thing for breakfast and lunch nearly every weekday. Routines are single decisions that eliminate a thousand future decisions and thus preserve your energy. A Time Budget is simply a means of documenting your planned routine for your time. Allow me to submit this simple definition for this new term:

TIME BUDGET: a plan for how you will spend your time in a given day

Sounds simple? It is. But don't let its simplicity fool you: this is *the key* to connecting the disconnected pieces of the puzzle for redeeming your time in a way that eliminates hurry. In this practice, you will build a Time Budget template for your ideal workday. In practice 2, you will see how to adjust your Time Budget template to accommodate the things that will inevitably conflict with your plan. And finally, in practice 3, you will examine how to protect your Time Budget with a Jesus-like approach to the word *no.*

A simple Time Budget is the key to connecting the disconnected pieces of the puzzle for redeeming your time.

At this point, you're probably wondering where your Time Budget will live physically. Don't worry; I'm not about to sell you a planner. Your Time Budget should live in your existing calendar system (Google Calendar, your daily planner, whatever). But let me stress this: it is *incredibly* helpful to make your Time Budget visually distinct from the appointments you have made with other people. Yes, I'm recommending that visually you make it look like you have two separate calendars: one for appointments with others (what you would traditionally call your "calendar"), and one for appointments you'll make with yourself for deep work, shallows and serendipity, and so on. That "second calendar" is your Time Budget.

The easiest way to distinguish these calendar items visually is by using different colors for each. On my calendar, my appointments with myself (my Time Budget) are in green, while my appointments with others are in red. For example, I have a "Call with Marybeth" on my calendar for 4:00 p.m. tomorrow. That appointment is colored red on my calendar. Also on my calendar tomorrow is a two-hour appointment with myself to write this book. That item is colored green on my calendar. It's super helpful to distinguish these two types of appointments visually because, at any time, you need to be able to see the fixed boundaries of your day. I promise you'll understand why fully in practice 2.

The remainder of this practice will show you how to build a Time Budget template for your ideal workday. If you'd prefer to work through this practice on paper, you can download a blank Time Budget template worksheet at JordanRaynor.com/RYT. If you'd prefer to work through this practice digitally, pick any future workday on your digital calendar and build your Time Budget template there. Don't worry if you already have appointments scheduled on those days. We will deal with those later. And at the end of this practice, once your template is finished, you'll edit each calendar item to make it recurring across each of your workdays.

Okay, so what goes into your Time Budget template? Pretty much everything we've learned about in this book. The following is a sequential list of items I would recommend you add to your Time Budget template.

Time in the Word

Place this rock onto your Time Budget first. As we saw in chapter 1, spending time in Scripture is *the* keystone habit for redeeming your time, and as we saw in chapter 3, it's a great way to start your day outside the kingdom of noise. Again, I recommend spending time in the Word in the morning, but what's far more important than *when* you do it is *that* you do it. Choose the time when you can most consistently engage with God's Word, and add it to your template. For me, that's in the morning between five and six.

Work

Just as the wisest financial budgeters operate with fixed budgets, we'd be wise to do the same with our working hours. As we saw in chapter 1, there will *always* be more work to do. We will all die with unfinished symphonies. That truth frees us to draw bright lines on our calendars for the amount of time we're willing to give our vocational callings each day.

How many hours should you budget for work? Of course, that's entirely up to you and your situation in life, but allow me to offer one piece of advice to recovering workaholics like me: numerous studies show that working more than 50 hours a week makes you *less* productive. In fact, in one study, Stanford professor Dr. John Pencavel found that "employee output falls sharply after a 50-hour work-week, and falls off a cliff after 55 hours—so much so that someone who puts in 70 hours *produces nothing more* with those extra 15 hours" (emphasis added).[25] That's just one more data point to support what we learned in chapter 6—that rest is counterintuitively productive or, at the very least, not *counter*productive.

Choose now when you will start and end your workday. For me, that's 7:30 a.m.–5:00 p.m. Whatever your ideal hours are, add them to your Time Budget template in a big single block of time called "Work." In a minute, we are going to replace this block with more specific budgets for our time at the office, but for now, this single block will do.

Morning Routine

This includes showering, getting the kids to school, and your commute. There's no need to budget each of these items individually. Just add a block that reads "Morning Routine" that extends to the start of your "Work" block. My morning routine extends from 6:00 a.m. (when I'm done reading the Word) to 7:30 a.m. (when I start my workday).

Evening Routine

Now it's time to budget your evening routine: the gap between the end of your workday and sleep. Of course, to determine the end of this block, you'll need to set a consistent target bedtime. As we saw in chapter 6, an eight-to-nine-hour sleep opportunity is nonnegotiable for nearly every person who desires to operate at 100 percent. So look at your Time Budget template and do the math. You've already budgeted when your day begins. Count back eight to nine hours, and that should mark when you are in bed sleeping. Before you go to bed, however, you will have an "Evening Routine" block from the end of your "Work" block until you go to bed.

First Block of Deep Work

I mentioned before that the "Work" block on your Time Budget was going to be replaced. Now that you've budgeted time for the Word,

5 AM	**Time in the Word** 5:00 a.m.–6:00 a.m.
6 AM	**Morning Routine** 6:00 a.m.–7:30 a.m.
7 AM	
8 AM	**Work** 7:30 a.m.–5:00 p.m.
9 AM	
10 AM	
11 AM	
12 PM	
1 PM	
2 PM	
3 PM	
4 PM	
5 PM	**Evening Routine** 5:00 p.m.–8:45 p.m.
6 PM	
7 PM	
8 PM	
9 PM	

your morning and evening routines, and sleep, it's time to delete the "Work" block in the middle. You are going to fill that space with a more specific budget for your ideal workday, starting with your first block of deep work, which you learned about in chapter 5.

If you recall, ninety minutes is the ideal length of time for blocks of deep work, but that may be unrealistic for you today. Even if you can budget only thirty minutes of depth each day, that's a terrific start in the right direction. Conversely, if you've spent years developing your focus muscles, you may find you're able to get away with blocks of deep work that are slightly longer than ninety minutes. Right now my personal Time Budget template calls for two two-hour blocks of deep work each morning.

Where should your first block of deep work appear on your Time Budget template? Let me reiterate a plea I first made in chapter 5: do *everything* you can to make your first block of deep work the first thing you do during your workday. If you listen to my podcast, *The Call to Mastery*, you know that *almost every one* of my world-class guests shares this habit. Why? Because these masters know that their first hours in the office are when their energy is the highest. Again, time management is really energy management, so our goal should be to do the work that requires the most energy (deep work) when our energy is highest (for most of us, at the beginning of the day) and save tasks that require the least amount of energy (shallow work) for when our energy is the lowest (at the end of the day).

Time management is really energy management.

Now, notice that I said *most* people's energy is highest in the morning. But that is certainly not true of everyone. In fact, a full 30 percent of people are "night-owls."[26] Contrary to what these people may have been told implicitly or explicitly, night-owlness does not equate to laziness. God has simply designed everyone with different internal clocks, or what scientists call "chronotypes," which are "strongly determined by genetics."[27] The problem is that our modern work and school calendars are built around morning birds, oftentimes leaving night owls at an unfair disadvantage.

So, what is a night owl to do? If you have a reasonable level of control of your schedule, do the *exact opposite* of what I'm suggesting in this practice. If it takes you until noon to feel fully energized, schedule your first block of deep work for the afternoon, and your shallow work and meetings in the morning.

Pull open your Time Budget template now and add a box titled "Deep Work Block #1" for whenever is right for you.

First Break

As we saw in chapter 6, scientists now understand that God has designed our bodies to pulse in ultradian cycles every other hour. If you've added a ninety-minute block of deep work to your Time Budget template, it's time to budget your first bi-hourly break. As I said before, I recommend fifteen to thirty minutes for these breaks, but go with whatever works for you. Currently, I take a forty-five-minute break after my first block of deep work to run and shower.

In chapter 6, practice 1, I listed a bunch of options for how to get the most energy out of these breaks, but now that we've established the concept of starting our day with depth, let me offer one more idea: if you commute, consider doing your first block of deep work from home while everyone else is stuck in traffic and use your drive to the office as your first break. Again, this is one of those double-win breaks I am such a fan of. You can avoid traffic *and* recharge your batteries for whatever comes next once you get into the office. Plus, when you're at home, it's harder for your team, boss, or coworkers to interrupt your cultivation of depth.

First Block for Checking Messages

As we saw in chapter 5, if you want to be fully present at work and home, you have to believe you have more control than you think over when you respond to incoming messages. That means choosing to check email and other messages a finite number of times a day. As I mentioned before, the *number* of times you check your messages doesn't matter nearly as much as the fact that *you* exert control over *when* your messages get checked.

So, when should you check them? Again, the answer is contingent on your personal energy level. If you're in the 30 percent of night owls, you may want to check email first thing in the morning. The rest of us should try to push our first block of email checking as late as our bosses, customers, and coworkers will enable us to.

On your Time Budget template, go ahead and add a block called "Check Messages" for the first time you'd like to process email and text messages. Ideally, this would be the same time you process your Inbox List in your Commitment Tracking System down to zero. If you're going to check messages more than once a day, don't worry about budgeting those other times just yet. We'll get to them soon.

Daily Review

The daily review is where you'll decide what you'll do tomorrow. I am going to show you exactly what this looks like in practice 2. For now, just pencil in fifteen minutes for it somewhere in your day. I recommend doing your daily review at or near the end of your workday, when there are no more opportunities for other people to reprioritize your to-do list for tomorrow.

Shallows and Serendipity

The wisdom of an emergency savings fund is widely accepted for financial budgeting. We need the same thing for our Time Budget. As we saw in chapter 5, a key to getting deep work done is to plan for the unplannable by creating space for shallow work, serendipitous encounters, and plain old interruptions and emergencies. We've already budgeted time for some shallow work (our first block of checking messages). Now's the time to budget for other types of shallow work that you expect in a typical workday (meetings, interruptions, urgent requests from clients, favors for friends, and so on).

I budget an hour and a half for "Shallows and Serendipity" at the end of my day. Depending on your type of work, you may need much more than that, and that's okay. Again, just like with email, the point isn't how much time you spend in shallow activities but that you exert control over when you spend time in the shallows.

Additional Blocks of Deep Work, Breaks, and Checking Messages

If you've budgeted time for all the elements we've discussed, you likely still have a healthy amount of white space on your Time Budget template. What do you do with it? Whatever is most appropriate for the callings, BHAGs, and OKRs you defined in chapter 4. If you're a programmer or writer, you'll likely want to budget a few more blocks of deep work. If you're in customer support or sales, you'll likely need to budget a few more blocks for checking messages. Whatever works for you works, but I'd encourage you not to leave any space open on your Time Budget template. Take the time now to ensure that "every minute has a name" in your ideal workday. Look at page 171 for a view of my completed Time Budget template. You can also download my personal Time Budget template as a PDF or a Google Calendar link at JordanRaynor.com/RYT.

Before we move on to practice 2, there are two more things you need to do. First, now that your Time Budget template is complete, go ahead and replicate it across every future workday. If you're using a digital calendar, edit each block of your Time Budget template to make it a recurring item on every one of your workdays. If you're using

5 AM	Time in the Word 5:00 a.m.–6:00 a.m.
6 AM	Morning Routine 6:00 a.m.–7:30 a.m.
7 AM	Deep Work Block #1 7:30 a.m.–9:30 a.m.
8 AM	
9 AM	
10 AM	Break #1 9:30 a.m.–10:15 a.m.
	Deep Work Block #2 10:15 a.m.–12:15 p.m.
11 AM	
12 PM	
	Break #2, 12:15 p.m.–12:30 p.m.
1 PM	Deep Work Block #3 12:30 p.m.–2:00 p.m.
2 PM	Break #3, 2:00 p.m.–2:15 p.m.
	Check Messages 2:15 p.m.–3:15 p.m.
3 PM	Daily Review, 3:15 p.m.–3:30 p.m.
	Shallows & Serendipity 3:30 p.m.–5:00 p.m.
4 PM	
5 PM	Evening Routine 5:00 p.m.–8:45 p.m.
6 PM	
7 PM	
8 PM	
9 PM	

the Time Budget worksheet that accompanies this chapter, replicate the budget you created however you see fit.*

Finally, take a minute to account for recurring exceptions to your Time Budget template. For example, let's say you've budgeted a block of deep work to start at 8:30 a.m. Monday through Friday, but on Tuesdays, you have a Bible study that will force you to push that block back to 9:00 a.m. Account for those known recurring exceptions now. What do you do with the nonrecurring exceptions, such as tomorrow's meeting with a prospective client or next week's birthday party? That question brings us to practice 2.

PRACTICE 2: ADJUST YOUR TIME BUDGET IN A DAILY REVIEW

Congratulations! You now have a budget for every minute of your ideal workweek. Now it's time to spend it. If practice 1 was analogous to deciding *how much* to spend on restaurants each month, this practice is the equivalent of choosing *which* restaurants to eat at each week. In this practice, you'll discover a simple plan for answering two questions:

1. How do you adjust your Time Budget on a daily basis to accommodate the things that will inevitably conflict with your plan?
2. How do you decide what to do during each scheduled block of deep work?

Those questions are answered with a simple daily review, which you can complete in fifteen minutes with these four steps.

Step 1: Pray

Remember that productivity prayer in chapter 1, practice 2? I pray it during almost every daily review to remind myself of what God's

---

* Again, you can download this at JordanRaynor.com/RYT.

Word says about work, time, and the role I have to play in God's mission in the world. I'd encourage you to do the same.

Step 2: Move Your Time Budget Blocks Around the Fixed Boundaries of Tomorrow

I promised you in practice 1 that making your Time Budget visually distinct from your normal calendar would be important. Now it's time to see why.

Let's say I'm doing my daily review on a Monday afternoon, planning out my Tuesday. By default, my recurring Time Budget has "Deep Work Block #1" scheduled for 7:30 a.m.–9:30 a.m. But now I see that I also have a "Call w/ Menekse" scheduled for 7:30 a.m.–8:30 a.m.

Because that call is an appointment with someone else, it is colored red on my calendar, while my block of deep work (an appointment with myself) is colored green. Everything in red represents the fixed boundaries of my day—the things I absolutely have to do based on commitments I have made to others. To honor those commitments, I need to rearrange the appointments with myself (my green Time Budget blocks) around my appointments with others (my red appointments). Once I've adjusted my Time Budget blocks around the fixed boundaries of tomorrow, my calendar will look something like the example on page 174.

5 AM	Time in the Word 5:00 a.m.–6:00 a.m.
6 AM	Morning Routine 6:00 a.m.–7:30 a.m.
7 AM	
8 AM	Call w/ Menekse 7:30 a.m.–8:30 a.m.
9 AM	Deep Work Block #1 8:30 a.m.–9:30 a.m.
10 AM	Break #1 9:30 a.m.–10:15 a.m.
11 AM	Deep Work Block #2 10:15 a.m.–12:15 p.m.
12 PM	
	Break #2, 12:15 p.m.–12:30 p.m.
1 PM	Deep Work Block #3 12:30 p.m.–2:00 p.m.
2 PM	Break #3, 2:00 p.m.–2:15 p.m.
	Check Messages 2:15 p.m.–3:15 p.m.
3 PM	Daily Review, 3:15 p.m.–3:30 p.m.
	Shallows & Serendipity, 3:30 p.m.–4:00 p.m.
4 PM	John and Jordan Sync Re: Illustrations, 4:00 p.m.–4:30 p.m.
	Call w/ DJ, 4:30 p.m.–5:00 p.m.
5 PM	Evening Routine 5:00 p.m.–8:45 p.m.
6 PM	
7 PM	
8 PM	
9 PM	

Step 3: Plug Projects into Your Time Budget

Now you know exactly how much time you have available tomorrow to work through your to-do list or, in the parlance of chapters 2 and 4, your Projects List and Actions List. With that information in hand, you can now schedule specific times to work on specific tasks. That's what this step of your daily review is all about. This is the beautiful moment in which your to-do list marries up with your Time Budget. How? By taking the projects you want to work on tomorrow and plugging them into specific blocks on your Time Budget, replacing the generic placeholder names in your template with something concrete.

For example, in my revised Time Budget for tomorrow, I now have "Deep Work Block #1" scheduled from 8:30 a.m.–9:30 a.m. Now is the time to replace that generic text with an actual project from my to-do list. For example, let's say that I know that the most important thing I can work on tomorrow is writing the rest of this chapter. I will replace the text "Deep Work Block #1" with "RYT: Writing" on my calendar. Once I've decided what I'll spend my time on in each of tomorrow's blocks, my calendar will look something like the example on page 176.

But hang on, Jordan. Didn't you say in chapter 2 that our calendars shouldn't serve as our to-do lists? Yes, and this is an important distinction. "RYT: Writing" isn't written as a well-defined, physical action. It's merely a *cue* to remind me of which item on my Actions List I have budgeted time to work on. When tomorrow morning rolls around, I will see this item on my calendar, which will trigger me to pull open my Commitment Tracking System (CTS) and work through my well-defined actions.

But, Jordan, how *do I decide which tasks to plug into my Time Budget? How do I decide what's* most *important to focus on for any given day?* This is where most people get stuck. The best tool I have found for answering this question is the Eisenhower Matrix, named after the American president who created a simple two-by-two chart to categorize his various work.[28]

5 AM	**Time in the Word** 5:00 a.m.–6:00 a.m.
6 AM	**Morning Routine** 6:00 a.m.–7:30 a.m.
7 AM	
8 AM	**Call w/ Menekse** 7:30 a.m.–8:30 a.m.
9 AM	**RYT: Writing** 8:30 a.m.–9:30 a.m.
	Break #1 9:30 a.m.–10:15 a.m.
10 AM	**RYT: Marketing Copy** 10:15 a.m.–12:15 p.m.
11 AM	
12 PM	
	Break #2, 12:15 p.m.–12:30 p.m.
1 PM	**Devotions** 12:30 p.m.–2:00 p.m.
2 PM	**Break #3, 2:00 p.m.–2:15 p.m.**
	Check Messages 2:15 p.m.–3:15 p.m.
3 PM	**Daily Review, 3:15 p.m.–3:30 p.m.**
	Shallows & Serendipity, 3:30 p.m.–4:00 p.m.
4 PM	**John and Jordan Sync Re: Illustrations, 4:00 p.m.–4:30 p.m.**
	Call w/ DJ, 4:30 p.m.–5:00 p.m.
5 PM	**Evening Routine** 5:00 p.m.–8:45 p.m.
6 PM	
7 PM	
8 PM	
9 PM	

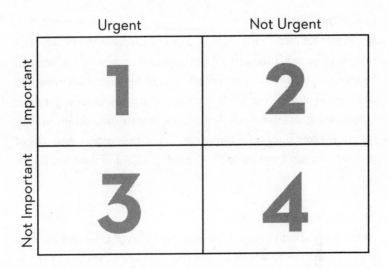

	Urgent	Not Urgent
Important	1	2
Not Important	3	4

We're not going to add items in quadrant 4 (Not Important & Not Urgent) into our Time Budgets. In fact, if you have any of these items on your to-do list or CTS, you should probably just delete them. Here, in priority order, are the types of to-dos we need to budget time for:

1. Important & Urgent
2. Important & Not Urgent
3. Not Important & Urgent

Or in the words of Saint Francis of Assisi, "Start by doing what's necessary, then what's possible, and suddenly you are doing the impossible."[29] If you did the work in chapter 2 and built your CTS, you can breathe a huge sigh of relief knowing that you don't have a dozen different places to look to identify your most important work. Your calendar and your CTS are *the only two tools* you need for discerning which to-dos fall in which quadrant of your matrix. With those tools in hand, where specifically can you look to identify what falls into these three categories?

IMPORTANT & URGENT

In chapter 2, I mentioned that due dates on to-dos in your CTS need to be kept sacred. This is why. During your daily review, you want to be able to quickly see what absolutely *must* get done tomorrow. Do you have to-dos in your CTS that are important and must get done tomorrow or sometime this week? Those are the first things to plug into your Time Budget for tomorrow. With these urgent items out of the way, you can move on to the second quadrant of the Eisenhower Matrix.

IMPORTANT & NOT URGENT

Next, view the active projects on your to-do list or CTS and use your best judgment as to which are the most important for you to tackle in the remaining time available tomorrow. In the example I shared previously, I had decided that writing the rest of this chapter was the most important thing for me to do tomorrow. That task isn't urgent (I'm writing this three months before my deadline), but it is incredibly important.

If you're like me, most of the items on your to-do list fall into this category of Important & Not Urgent. They are actions that will help you make meaningful progress toward the goals you defined in chapter 4, but nobody is holding your feet to the fire to complete them by a certain date. So, they are constantly being prioritized behind urgent things clamoring for your attention.

The irony, of course, is that if we dealt with Important & Not Urgent things more frequently, we would have far less urgent things on our plate. If you're constantly getting bogged down by urgent administrative tasks, the highest-leverage thing you can do might be to hire an assistant. But because "Draft job description for assistant" isn't an urgent task, it gets pushed off, only making the problem worse. Sound familiar? If you share this problem, consider these words from Timothy Keller: "Self-control is the ability to do the important thing rather than the urgent thing."[30]

If during your daily review you're still having a hard time discerning what's most important on your to-do list, ask yourself one of my all-time favorite questions: *Which problem, once solved, is going to make most of my other problems easier to solve or disappear entirely?*[31] Underline that question, highlight it, or write it on a Post-it Note near your desk. I promise that question will prioritize your work more times than not.

Which problem, once solved, is going to make most of my other problems easier to solve or disappear entirely?

Okay, once you've added your Important & Urgent tasks and Important & Not Urgent tasks to your Time Budget, there's one more category of tasks to consider budgeting time for tomorrow.

NOT IMPORTANT & URGENT

Before you schedule time to do these tasks, try your hardest *not* to do them. This can be done by delegating the task to someone else* or attempting to renegotiate the commitment with whomever delegated the task to you. But even if you don't agree with your boss's perspective, if he or she says a task is important, it's important, because serving our employers well is a biblical command (see Ephesians 6:5–8; Colossians 3:22–25).

If you have tasks you deem Not Important & Urgent on your to-do list, be encouraged that most of these tasks take very little time. Examples include categorizing expenses in QuickBooks or submitting your time sheet to your boss. Here's my advice on how to handle small tasks like these that take only a few minutes to complete: Don't schedule them. Don't add them to your Time Budget. Whenever you have a few minutes free throughout your day, do them then.

---

*Need help deciding what you should delegate and how to delegate well? Check out the video on this topic at JordanRaynor.com/RYT.

By now all the generic names in your Time Budget should be replaced with concrete reminders of actions you plan to take tomorrow. There is just one more step for completing your daily review.

Step 4: Check for Ample Breaks and Margin

To be unrushed like Jesus, we must develop the habit of ensuring we have plenty of breaks and margin built into our calendars. This is *essential* for eliminating hurry throughout the day, which is exactly what we're after as we attempt to redeem our time in the model of our Redeemer.

Got a coffee meeting tomorrow that's a fifteen-minute drive from the office? Budget thirty minutes into your Time Budget to get there. Think email is going to take you forty-five minutes? Budget sixty.

We are all *terrible* at estimating how long it will take to do something.[32] Don't just be cognizant of this fact; *do* something about it. Specifically, pack plenty of breaks and margin into your Time Budget, overestimating how long it will take you to do everything, especially *new* things.*

PRACTICE 3: PROTECT YOUR TIME BUDGET WITH A UNIQUE APPROACH TO "NO"

Throughout this chapter, I've been comparing the concept of budgeting time to budgeting money, so let's extend that analogy one last time. If your friends ask you to go out to dinner tonight but you have zero dollars left in your bank account, you have to say no or risk going into debt. Similarly, when it comes to budgeting our time, we must develop the skill of saying no to demands on our time that will put

---

*Want to vastly improve your ability to estimate how long it will take to complete certain projects and tasks? Watch the video on how I track my time and use the data to update my Time Budgets at JordanRaynor.com/RYT.

us in the red territory of hurry. It's not enough to just build our Time Budget templates and adjust them each day (see practices 1 and 2). To eliminate hurry, we must learn how to *protect* our Time Budgets with a unique approach to the powerful word *no*.

Why a unique approach? Because secular thinking on this topic doesn't always align with Jesus's example in the Gospels. Author and TED speaker Derek Sivers summarized modern thinking on this two-letter word: "When deciding whether to do something, if you feel anything less than 'Wow! That would be amazing! Absolutely!' . . . then say 'no.' "[33] The appeal of extreme criteria like this is obvious, as we all need tools to be more selective about what we're saying yes to. But "It's gotta be amazing or it's a no" isn't the answer, as this mindset is entirely self-serving and thus out of step with the example of Christ.

A scene recorded in the gospel of Matthew illustrates my point. In Matthew 14:1–12, we learn about how Jesus heard the news that his beloved friend and cousin John the Baptist had been beheaded. The first half of verse 13 tells us that "when Jesus heard what had happened, he withdrew by boat privately to a solitary place." Understandably, all Jesus wanted to do in that moment was be alone. But the crowds wouldn't let him.

The second half of verse 13 tells us that "hearing of this, the crowds followed him on foot from the towns." So, Jesus is out there in his boat, trying to get away from it all. The *last* thing he wants to do is spend time among a crowd of people. But Jesus can't hide from his celebrity. Hordes of people are running along the shore, trying to wave him in. What will he do? Surely he isn't thinking of the crowd's incessant request, *Wow! That would be amazing! Absolutely!* And certainly if there were ever a time when it would have been understandable for Jesus to say no to the people's request, it's right here in this scene. But remarkably, Jesus *doesn't* say no. Verse 14 says that "when Jesus landed and saw a large crowd, he had compassion on them and healed their sick."

Now, as we already saw in chapter 4, Jesus didn't always say yes to requests like these. All throughout the Gospels, we see him saying no (see Luke 4:38–44; 5:15–16; 10:38–42; John 6:23–27). Sometimes Jesus said yes to requests for his time, while other times he said no. So, where does that leave us? How can we discern when we're called to say no, in an effort to protect our Time Budgets, and when we're called to say yes?

Like with so many other questions in life, I don't believe there are always right and wrong answers to this question. Redeeming our time requires a lot of prayer, wisdom, and courage to exercise our God-given freedom to choose. That said, there are several questions that I find extremely helpful when deciding whether to say yes or no to a request for my time. I'm hoping these questions will be helpful to you as well. In the following section, I have shared each of these questions organized into the two buckets that nearly every request for our time falls into: *favors* (things that primarily bring *others* value) and *opportunities* (things that primarily bring *us* value).

Four Questions to Ask Before Saying Yes to Favors

QUESTION #1: AM I THE BEST PERSON TO SAY YES TO THIS REQUEST?

Let's face it: it's flattering to be asked for help. When someone requests time to access our skills or knowledge, that person is signaling that we have some level of qualification to serve. But oftentimes, we aren't the *most* qualified person we know to help with a particular favor, and saying yes can actually be a disservice to the person requesting our help.

For example, if you asked me to help you build a tree house, I would say no because I am the *least* handy person on earth. Saying yes would fail to serve you well. Or let's say an elder in your church asks you to serve on the church's finance committee but you're terrible at math. The most loving thing you can do in that scenario is say no to the request and point the elder to someone else in the church who excels in finance.

Is the favor you're being asked to provide in line with the callings you identified in chapter 4? If not, consider saying no to the request.

QUESTION #2: IS THIS THE MOST GENEROUS USE OF MY TIME?

At first glance, saying yes to a request for your time may look generous. But oftentimes, yeses are far less generous than they seem, as every yes forces you to say no to many other people you could be serving with that time.

Let's pretend I'm traveling to Washington, DC, and I email bestselling author Mark Batterson, asking if he'd be willing to meet up for an hour-long coffee. The most generous thing Batterson can do with that hour of time is *not* saying yes to my request—it's saying no so he can focus on writing his next book, which will serve me *and* thousands of other people well. In the words of Batterson himself, "The way I see it, books are my way of spending five hours with anybody, anywhere, anytime. . . . There is tremendous value in meeting with someone one on one, but my time is multiplied only by a factor of one. With books, my time is multiplied by the total number of readers."[34]

Many times, saying no to a request for a favor is the most generous thing you can do—not for the requester, but for the *others* you're called to serve with that time.

QUESTION #3: WOULD I SAY YES TO A HUNDRED SIMILAR REQUESTS FOR MY TIME?

For better or worse, every yes we give contributes to the building of a habit, making it easier and more routine to say yes to similar requests in the future. When you're considering whether or not to say yes to someone's request to grab a cup of coffee, you're not just deciding if you'll say yes to *this* coffee but you're also deciding if you want to develop the habit of accepting a hundred coffee meetings *like* this one in the future.

QUESTION #4: DO I HAVE ROOM IN MY TIME BUDGET TO SAY YES TO THIS FAVOR?

In chapter 5, we saw why we need to confine serendipitous encounters and favors to predefined places on our calendars. In this chapter, you created space for these types of activities when you added a block for "Shallows and Serendipity" to your Time Budget template. This makes it *much* easier to say yes or no to requests for your time that fall into the category of favors. If you answered yes to questions 1 through 3, look at your Time Budget to see if you have room to say yes to this request for your time. If you do, great! Say yes and serve that person well with that time. If you don't have time available, protect your Time Budget by delivering a "generous no."

In a minute, I'll provide you with some tips for saying no generously and tactfully. But first, now that we've explored four questions to help us decide whether to say yes or no to *favors,* we need to collect a set of questions that will help us discern how to respond to unexpected *opportunities.*

Four Questions to Ask Before Saying Yes to Opportunities

QUESTION #1: IS THIS OPPORTUNITY ALIGNED WITH MY GOALS?

The whole purpose of chapter 4 was to set goals that help prioritize your to-do list and where you spend your time. If an unexpected opportunity comes your way, your first question should be whether or not the opportunity is aligned with the goals you've set for this season of life. If it's not, your default response should be no. Trust me, I know that this is tough, *especially* if an opportunity appears to be particularly great. That's why I love to ask this second question.

QUESTION #2: THIS IS A REALLY GREAT OPPORTUNITY . . . FOR WHAT?

I wish I could take credit for this killer question, but I can't. I give full credit to Emily P. Freeman, who said this:

The phrase "It's a great opportunity" is not actually a complete sentence. . . . A great opportunity to . . . *what*? The literal definition of *opportunity* is "a set of circumstances that makes it possible to do something." If it's true that this thing is actually a great opportunity for you, you have to be able to finish the sentence.[35]

Opportunities that aren't attached to some meaningful end *aren't* opportunities—they are simply possibilities that stir up frantic excitement. Again, if an opportunity isn't aligned with your goals, it's probably not a good use of your time.

Opportunities that aren't attached to some meaningful end aren't opportunities—they are simply possibilities that stir up frantic excitement.

But, Jordan, this is a once-in-a-lifetime opportunity! I used to believe in once-in-a-lifetime opportunities too. But after years of seeing God graciously provide opportunities that kept topping the previous ones, I gave up. Sir Richard Branson once said that "opportunities are like buses—there's always another one coming!"[36] In my experience, that's exactly right.

As I was writing this chapter, I received an invitation to attend an *amazing* event. The guest list was top-notch, the location was magnificent, and everything was paid for. Who *wouldn't* want to say yes to that type of opportunity? Later, as I was explaining the event to my wife, I excitedly said, "It's *such* a great opportunity," to which she replied as if on cue, "For what?" I couldn't answer the question. After some soul searching, I realized I was trying to *look* good rather than *do* good with my time, which brings me to my next question for discerning opportunities.

QUESTION #3: AM I TRYING TO *DO* GOOD OR MAKE MYSELF *LOOK* GOOD?

Kevin DeYoung gets credit for this question. Remember why you care about redeeming your time. It's all about doing more good works for others, *not* a means of making ourselves look good. If we're honest, looking good is why we say yes to many opportunities. It's what I was doing when I was considering attending the event I mentioned previously. I wanted to attend because the guest list was amazing and I wanted to sit at the cool-kids' table. So lame. Thankfully, I have a wife who is able to spot my insecurities and keep me focused on doing work that serves others rather than my ego. Remember, because of the gospel and our status as adopted children of God, we have no need to "look good." We are sons and daughters of the King, called to redeem our time wisely for his purposes.[37]

QUESTION #4: *WHAT* WILL I SAY NO TO?

When presented with an opportunity, the question you have to answer isn't "*Will* I say no?" It's "*What* will I say no to?" Saying yes to writing this book meant saying no to writing a book on one of the three other topics I was considering. In the words of former Apple design chief Jony Ive, "There are a thousand no's for every yes."[38]

As we saw in chapter 3, we don't think in terms of cost-benefit analysis nearly enough when it comes to our time. We ask questions like, "Is going to this conference a good use of my time?" That's a bad question. We need to ask questions that weigh value *relative* to cost, including opportunity cost. A better question to ask of the conference would be, "Is attending this conference a good use of my time *compared to* all the other things I could be doing with that time?" The law of time and trade-offs requires that we always say no to something.

I hope those questions help you discern when to say yes to requests for your time and when to say no. If you're like me, you need way more help saying no than saying yes. So, once you've made a decision to say no to protect your Time Budget and eliminate hurry, how do you deliver that no in the most generous way? Here are three tips.

Three Tips for Delivering a Generous No

TIP #1: DELAY YOUR RESPONSE

You just received a text with an invitation to one of those once-in-a-lifetime opportunities. Let me encourage you to sit on the invitation for twenty-four hours before you say yes. How many times have you agreed to do something, only to regret your commitment as the day approaches? Proverbs 20:25 says, "It is a trap to dedicate something rashly and only later to consider one's vows." Disciplining yourself to delay responses to all opportunities helps avoid this mistake. Plus, almost all opportunities lose some of their luster after the initial dopamine rush wears off.

Delaying your response to requests for your time is much easier in email and texts than it is when you're talking to someone on a call or in person, in which case I try my hardest to punt on a response if there's any chance I will say yes. I'll say, "Let me check my calendar and get back to you," or I'll utter every husband's favorite excuse: "Let me check with my wife."

Now, if you *know* you're going to say no, there's no reason to delay your answer. In the words of former Chick-fil-A president Jimmy Collins, "It is kindness to refuse immediately what you eventually intend to deny."[39] In these cases, the speed in which you say no is part of how you deliver your no generously.

TIP #2: ENCOURAGE, DECLINE, AND HELP

You just received an email from a friend of a friend you've never met. This second-degree connection is moving to your city and wants to meet up for coffee to discuss job opportunities in the area. This request for your time falls squarely into the category of favor. Assuming you're not a headhunter, you're probably not the best person to help your friend's friend, and this meeting is almost certainly not the most generous use of your time. But is there a way to say no in a generous way that serves this person well? I think there is! Here's the message I would send:

> Welcome to the neighborhood! You're going to love it here.
>
> Unfortunately, my schedule is fully committed, so I will not be able to meet up for coffee.
>
> That said, if you have specific questions about employers in the area, I'd be more than happy to answer your questions via email!

This message has three components that I recommend including anytime you want to deliver a generous no.

Encourage: The first line of this email serves to encourage the sender simply by responding to his or her request and affirming the person's decision to move to your city.

Decline: The second paragraph of this email unequivocally declines this person's request for coffee by leveraging one of my favorite terms: "fully committed." I love how the Four Seasons uses "fully committed" to describe when they have no rooms available in their hotels. As Dee Ann Turner, Chick-fil-A's former vice president of talent, explained,

> [Four Seasons doesn't] say to the guest, "we have no vacancy" or "we are sold out." In that simple phrase, the guest is informed that the Four Seasons is fully committed to serving their guests, and if they have no rooms to offer on this stay, they hope you will know they are fully committed to serving you during a future stay.[40]

You can communicate this same powerful message with this simple two-word phrase as you decline requests for your time.

One more thing before we look at the third component of this email response. You'll notice that this response is emphatic and leaves zero wiggle room. When you use phrases like, "I won't be able to meet up *anytime soon*," you are asking the person to follow up at some point in the future, thus requiring you to expend energy considering the request again.

Help: The third and final paragraph of my response makes a clear offer of help relevant to the person's original request. This is what makes this no generous! If someone is going to take the time to ask for my help, I may not give anywhere close to the full amount of time he or she is requesting, but I will always try to find a way to serve the individual in some other capacity. Offering to answer questions via email is my favorite way to accomplish this. In the coffee example, instead of spending an hour and a half away from the office for a coffee meeting, you can spend five minutes answering that person's specific questions via email. You save time, the individual gets the answers he or she is looking for, and everybody wins.

If someone is going to take the time to ask for my help, I may not give anywhere close to the full amount of time he or she is requesting, but I will always try to find a way to serve the individual in some other capacity.

TIP #3: ACCEPT BEING MISUNDERSTOOD

After you deliver a generous no following the "encourage, decline, help" framework, prepare to be misunderstood. That, of course, is a real potential consequence of protecting your Time Budget. But in my experience, *way* more people articulate respect than disappointment for my generous no. Why? Because they want to get better at protecting *their* time too. In an odd way, your delivery of a generous no shows them how.

Are there times when people express disappointment in my decisions to say no? Sure, but I've grown to be okay with that, because we aren't called to be everywhere every time. We're not even called to be understood. Jesus certainly wasn't.

What *are* we called to? We're called to model Jesus's example of counting the cost and eliminating hurry from our schedules. We're called to glorify the Father by doing good works for others. We're called to reflect Jesus by being purposeful, present, and wildly productive. In short, we're called to redeem our time.

CONNECTING THE PUZZLE PIECES

With this final chapter, I'm confident that you now have the tools to connect the seven biblical principles of this book together in a comprehensive system that enables you to be purposeful, present, and productive at work and home. But here's the thing: if you made it to the end of this book, you are probably a high-achieving, disciplined person like me. Our God-given discipline is undoubtedly a blessing, but it can also become an idolatrous curse. So, before you close this book, please join me in the following brief epilogue on "the dark side of discipline."

THE DARK SIDE OF DISCIPLINE

f you made it through all this book's seven principles and thirty-two practices, you might be thinking in a less-than-admiring way, *Wow, Jordan is disciplined.*

It's true that I am incredibly disciplined with my time, and I make no apologies to that end. Why? Because as we've seen throughout this book, Jesus himself was crazy disciplined with his time here on earth. He was intentional about glorifying the Father by "finishing the work [he was given] to do" (John 17:4). Jesus's example shows us that discipline is a virtue, and this is a theme the writers of Scripture carry throughout the New Testament. For example, the apostle Paul wrote,

> Don't you know that when people run on the race-track everybody runs, but only one person gets the prize? Run in such a way that you'll win it. Everyone who goes in for athletics exercises self-discipline in everything. They do it to gain a crown that perishes; we do it for an imperishable one. Well then: I don't run in an aimless fashion! I don't box like someone punching the air! No: I give my body rough treatment, and make it my slave, in case, after announcing the message to others, I myself should end up being disqualified. (1 Corinthians 9:24–27, NTE)

As Christ followers, we don't run through life "in an aimless fashion." We are called to "self-discipline in everything," exhibiting what

Paul also calls "self-control" in the fruit of the Spirit (see Galatians 5:22–23). Discipline is a by-product of a Spirit-filled, Christlike life.

But as with any good thing, we can easily make discipline an *ultimate* thing and thus turn it into an idol. Discipline is a gift, but it can also be a curse. That's my challenge; I pray it won't be yours. So, as you wrap up this book filled with disciplined practices to help you redeem your time, let me encourage you to be on the lookout for two signs that you've crossed over to the dark side of discipline and turned this good gift into an idol.

First, we can know discipline has become an idol when *we are unable to extend grace to others who are less disciplined than ourselves.* In his exceptional book *The Prodigal God,* Timothy Keller shows how many of us are like the elder brother in Jesus's parable of the prodigal son. Unlike younger brothers, who build their self-image around freedom and rebellion, "elder brothers base their self-images on being hardworking, or moral, or members of an elite clan, or extremely smart and savvy."[1] Sounds like me and probably you if this book for "hardworking . . . smart and savvy" people has resonated with you. But here's the problem: elder-brotherness "inevitably leads to feeling superior to those who don't have those same qualities."[2]

Can I be real a second?* That last line stings me to the core, because on my worst days, that's me. If someone shares that he or she is drowning in emails or struggling to make time to be in the Word every day, my first inclination might be to help, but I'll also likely feel a tinge of pride that I am more disciplined and better than my friend. If someone shows up late to a meeting or forgets to do something because his or her Commitment Tracking System isn't nearly as robust as mine, I can find myself seething with self-righteous anger that attempts to mask the fact that I, too, have made the exact same mistakes.

Can you relate to what I'm talking about? I don't think I'm on an island here. If this is part of what the dark side of discipline looks like

* For just a millisecond?

for you, let me remind you (and myself) that the root cause of our failure to extend grace to the less disciplined people in our lives is a forgetfulness of the gospel. We can't forget that *everything* we have—including our ability to be disciplined as we redeem our time—has been graciously given to us. James 1:17 says that "every good and perfect gift is from above, coming down from the Father." Our ability to be disciplined in redeeming our time is a gift of grace, just like salvation, "so that no one can boast" (Ephesians 2:9).

> *Everything we have—including our ability to be disciplined as we redeem our time—has been graciously given to us.*

I can't take credit for the wisdom I have shared in this book. Over the years, God has graciously brought books, mentors, software, and systems into my life to help me redeem my time for his glory. I did nothing but willfully participate in the process, and even that I can't take credit for, as God is the one who allows me to wake up each morning to do this work. Every word of this book has been graciously given to me. Now the Lord has used me to graciously share this knowledge with you. My prayer is that you and I will use the practices from this book to be time redeemers who extend grace to others who have yet to be graced with the knowledge and tools we have been given.

Of course, being hard on others isn't the only way we can know we've crossed over to the dark side of discipline. The second sign that we've made discipline an idol is that *we are unable to extend grace to ourselves.* I can be hard on myself if I get only two hours of deep work done instead of four. I can get mad if the baby is up all night and I fail to get my precious eight hours of sleep. I can even find myself depressed if I fall short of hitting my quarterly goals. Here again, the solution is the gospel, which is why I will end this book the same way I began it: by reminding us that the gospel frees us from the *need* to be productive. God doesn't need us to finish our to-do lists. He loves and accepts us no matter how many good things we do and no matter how productive we are.

God doesn't need us to finish our to-do lists. He loves and accepts us no matter how many good things we do and no matter how productive we are.

Read 1 Corinthians 9:25 one more time: "Everyone who goes in for athletics exercises self-discipline in everything. They do it to gain a crown that perishes; we do it for an imperishable one" (NTE). Our crowns are *imperishable.* Yes, our crowns might have more or less jewels in them, based on how we steward this life, and that should motivate us to redeem our time, just as it motivated Paul. But our entrance into God's kingdom—our position as princes and princesses—is secure forever. May that security lead us to be "self-discipline[d] in everything" as we seek to redeem our time. May we be people who, like Jesus, are purposeful, present, and *wildly* productive on behalf of our King.

ACKNOWLEDGMENTS

Dozens of people deserve to have their name on the cover of this book alongside mine. But my publisher assured me that would make for a hideous cover, so I will thank some of those people here.

To Kara, my beautiful bride: you're always ten times more confident in my work than I am, and for that I am eternally grateful. Thank you for showing me that you genuinely believe in me and this work we get to do together.

To Ellison, Kate, and Emery: I treasure every minute the Lord has given me with you. Thank you for being as excited about this book as a six-, four-, and one-year-old can be.

To Kayla Taylor, Jenna Fortier, Chris Perry, RJ Taylor, Hollie Smith, Johanna Vann, and Allie Wood: I am constantly amazed and grateful for the extreme "talent density" at Jordan Raynor & Company. You are the best team an entrepreneur could ask for. It is my joy to co-labor with you every single day. Thank you for the countless hours you have put in to bringing this message into the world.

To my agent, DJ Snell: looking back, you had little reason to bet on me as an unknown first-time author. I'll never forget your confidence in me. Thank you for partnering with me in this and every project!

To Becky Nesbitt: I'm thrilled we get to work on (at least) two more books together (Lord willing). Thank you for "killing my darlings" in such a gracious way and for helping me make the very best book.

To the entire team at WaterBrook Multnomah, but especially

Campbell Wharton, Tina Constable, Laura Barker, Douglas Mann, Brett Benson, Lori Addicott, Abby DeBenedittis, and Cara Iverson: you all are a dream to work with. Thank you for your enthusiasm for this book and my mission.

To Jessica Penick, Jordan Wiseman, Casey Case, and the entire team at YouVersion: this book literally wouldn't exist without you opening your platform to our content, including the "Time Management Principles from God's Word" plan that inspired *Redeeming Your Time*. Thank you for allowing my team to partner with you in equipping the church to engage with the Word daily.

To Chris Basham, David Block, Menekse Stewart, Hanna Shiplett, John Brandon, Jason Snow, Jillian Jenkins, Greg Kester, Donna Bucher, Jeni Englund, Sharon Justice, Melody Keller, Larry Tyler, and Sheri White: this is a much better book because of your early feedback. Thank you for helping me serve future readers well!

To my launch team: I dare someone to show me a more engaged, more passionate launch team than you all. You truly are the best. Thank you for your enthusiastic participation in our work of inspiring every Christian to do their most exceptional work for the glory of God and the good of others.

To The Church at Odessa: I love you all deeply and am so grateful for your support of my work.

To Aaron Sorkin and Lin-Manuel Miranda: thank you for the never-ending supply of *West Wing* and *Hamilton* Easter eggs to keep my fellow fans smirking as they read these pages.

To my Redeemer: thank you for loving me "no matter how many good things I do and no matter how many bad things I do." I owe you everything. *Soli Deo gloria.*

NOTES

Introduction: The Solution to Being Swamped

1. Matt Perman, *What's Best Next: How the Gospel Transforms the Way You Get Things Done* (Grand Rapids, MI: Zondervan, 2014), 120.
2. "1805. exagorazó," *Strong's Concordance,* Bible Hub, https://biblehub.com/greek/1805.htm.
3. Timothy Keller, "Wisdom and Sabbath Rest," Redeemer City to City, July 13, 2021, https://redeemercitytocity.com/articles-stories/wisdom-and-sabbath-rest.
4. Jen Wilkin, *None Like Him: 10 Ways God Is Different from Us (and Why That's a Good Thing)* (Wheaton, IL: Crossway, 2016), 74.

Chapter 1: Start with the Word

1. "William Wilberforce," The Wilberforce School, www.wilberforceschool.org/updated-about-us/william-wilberforce.
2. Eric Metaxas, *Amazing Grace: William Wilberforce and the Heroic Campaign to End Slavery* (San Francisco: HarperCollins, 2007), xvii.
3. Metaxas, *Amazing Grace,* xvii.
4. Metaxas, *Amazing Grace,* xvi, 52.
5. William Wilberforce, quoted in Metaxas, *Amazing Grace,* 54.
6. Metaxas, *Amazing Grace,* 59–60.
7. Metaxas, *Amazing Grace,* xvi.
8. Wilberforce, quoted in Metaxas, *Amazing Grace,* 52.
9. Metaxas, *Amazing Grace,* 67.
10. Wilberforce, quoted in Metaxas, *Amazing Grace,* 64.
11. Metaxas, *Amazing Grace,* 67.

12. Metaxas, *Amazing Grace,* 65.

13. Os Guinness, *Carpe Diem Redeemed: Seizing the Day, Discerning the Times* (Downers Grove, IL: InterVarsity, 2019), 11.

14. Guinness, *Carpe Diem,* 9.

15. Edward Banfield, quoted in "The Key to Long-Term Success," Brian Tracy International, www.briantracy.com/blog/leadership-success/the-key-to-long-term-success.

16. Stephen R. Covey, *The 7 Habits of Highly Effective People,* 30th anniversary ed. (New York: Simon & Schuster, 2020), 146.

17. Austin Burkhart, "'Avodah': What It Means to Live a Seamless Life of Work, Worship, and Service," Institute for Faith, Work and Economics, March 31, 2015, https://tifwe.org/avodah-a-life-of-work-worship-and-service/.

18. Arthur Miller, *Death of a Salesman,* Viking Critical Library, ed. Gerald Weales (New York: Penguin Books, 1996), 162.

19. Jen Wilkin, *None Like Him: 10 Ways God Is Different from Us (and Why That's a Good Thing)* (Wheaton, IL: Crossway, 2016), 72.

20. Leslie Odom Jr. et al., "The Room Where It Happens," by Lin-Manuel Miranda, *Hamilton: An American Musical,* Atlantic Records, 2015.

21. Phillipa Soo et al., "That Would Be Enough," by Lin-Manuel Miranda, *Hamilton: An American Musical,* Atlantic Records, 2015.

22. Karl Rahner, *Servants of the Lord* (New York: Herder and Herder, 1968), 152.

23. Metaxas, *Amazing Grace,* xix.

24. Metaxas, *Amazing Grace,* 280.

25. C. S. Lewis, *Mere Christianity* (New York: HarperCollins, 2015), 136–37.

26. Wilkin, *None Like Him,* 79.

27. Timothy Keller, *Walking with God Through Pain and Suffering* (New York: Penguin Books, 2013), 46.

28. Lisa Miller, "Pope's Book: A Lifetime of Learning," *Newsweek,* May 20, 2007, www.newsweek.com/popes-book-lifetime-learning-101009.

29. N. T. Wright, *God and the Pandemic: A Christian Reflection on the Coronavirus and Its Aftermath* (Grand Rapids, MI: Zondervan, 2020), 32.

30. Floyd Flake, in foreword to Eric Metaxas, *Amazing Grace: William Wilberforce and the Heroic Campaign to End Slavery* (San Francisco: HarperCollins, 2007), x.

31. Wilkin, *None Like Him,* 80.

32. D. Martyn Lloyd-Jones, *Studies in the Sermon on the Mount* (Grand Rapids, MI: Eerdmans, 2000), 96.

33. Matt Perman, *What's Best Next: How the Gospel Transforms the Way You Get Things Done* (Grand Rapids, MI: Zondervan, 2014), 14.

34. "2041. ergon," *Strong's Concordance,* Bible Hub, https://biblehub.com/greek/2041.htm.

35. John Piper, *Don't Waste Your Life,* Group Study Edition (Wheaton, IL: Crossway, 2018), 138.

36. Timothy Keller, *Encounters with Jesus: Unexpected Answers to Life's Biggest Questions* (New York: Penguin Books, 2013), 175.

37. Kevin DeYoung, *Crazy Busy: A (Mercifully) Short Book About a (Really) Big Problem* (Wheaton, IL: Crossway, 2013), 54.

38. John Mark Comer, *The Ruthless Elimination of Hurry* (Colorado Springs, CO: WaterBrook, 2019), 103–4.

39. Comer, *Ruthless Elimination,* 102.

40. Emily P. Freeman, *The Next Right Thing: A Simple, Soulful Practice for Making Life Decisions* (Grand Rapids, MI: Revell, 2019), 85.

41. Perman, *What's Best Next,* 51.

42. Charles Duhigg, *The Power of Habit: Why We Do What We Do in Life and Business* (New York: Random House, 2014), 100.

43. Duhigg, *Power of Habit,* 100.

44. See Timothy Keller, *Prayer: Experiencing Awe and Intimacy with God* (New York: Penguin Books, 2016), 90–91.

45. Bill Clinton, quoted in "The 1992 Campaign: Verbatim; Heckler Stirs Clinton Anger: Excerpts from the Exchange," *New York Times,* March 28, 1992, www.nytimes.com/1992/03/28/us/1992-campaign -verbatim-heckler-stirs-clinton-anger-excerpts-exchange.html.

46. Martin Luther, quoted in Covey, *7 Habits,* 348.

47. Comer, *Ruthless Elimination,* 136.

48. Comer, *Ruthless Elimination,* 136.

49. Phil Knight, *Shoe Dog: A Memoir by the Creator of Nike* (New York: Scribner, 2018), 179.

50. C. S. Lewis, *The Lion, the Witch and the Wardrobe* (New York: Harper-Collins, 2002), 87.

Chapter 2: Let Your Yes Be Yes

1. N. T. Wright, *Paul for Everyone: 1 Corinthians,* New Testament for Everyone (Louisville, KY: Westminster John Knox, 2004), 175–76.
2. Roy F. Baumeister and John Tierney, *Willpower: Rediscovering the Greatest Human Strength* (New York: Penguin Books, 2012), 81.
3. Baumeister and Tierney, *Willpower,* 81.
4. Baumeister and Tierney, *Willpower,* 83.
5. Baumeister and Tierney, *Willpower,* 84.
6. David Allen, *Getting Things Done: The Art of Stress-Free Productivity* (New York: Penguin Books, 2015), 14.
7. David Allen, *Getting Things Done,* 24–25.
8. Daniel J. Levitin, *The Organized Mind: Thinking Straight in the Age of Information Overload* (New York: Dutton, 2014), 68–69.
9. Allen, *Getting Things Done,* 25.
10. "Man on Cusp of Having Fun Suddenly Remembers Every Single One of His Responsibilities," *Onion,* May 30, 2013, https://local.the onion.com/man-on-cusp-of-having-fun-suddenly-remembers-every-sing-1819575063.
11. Ryder Carroll, *The Bullet Journal Method: Track the Past, Order the Present, Design the Future* (New York: Portfolio, 2018), 37.
12. David Allen, *Ready for Anything: 52 Productivity Principles for Getting Things Done* (New York: Penguin Books, 2004), 19.
13. Billy Joel, "A Matter of Trust," by Billy Joel, *The Bridge,* Columbia, 1985.
14. Jen Wilkin, *In His Image: 10 Ways God Calls Us to Reflect His Character* (Wheaton, IL: Crossway, 2018), 107.
15. Levitin, *The Organized Mind,* 69.
16. Matt Perman, *What's Best Next: How the Gospel Transforms the Way You Get Things Done* (Grand Rapids, MI: Zondervan, 2014), 119–20.
17. Allen, *Getting Things Done,* 22.
18. Cal Newport, *Digital Minimalism: Choosing a Focused Life in a Noisy World* (New York: Portfolio, 2019), 126.

19. Stephen R. Covey, *The 7 Habits of Highly Effective People*, 30th anniversary ed. (New York: Simon & Schuster, 2020), 113.

20. Allen, *Getting Things Done*, 38.

21. Allen, *Getting Things Done*, 42.

22. Kristen Bell, "The Next Right Thing," by Kristen Anderson-Lopez and Robert Lopez, *Frozen II*, Wonderland Music Company, 2019.

23. Martin Luther King Jr., quoted in Marian Wright Edelman, "Kids First!," *Mother Jones* magazine, May/June 1991, 77.

24. Allen, *Getting Things Done*, 260.

25. Allen, *Getting Things Done*, 107.

Chapter 3: Dissent from the Kingdom of Noise

1. Courtney Vinopal, "Activists Reflect on 1963 March on Washington Amid Renewed Calls to Address Racial Injustice," *PBS NewsHour*, August 31, 2020, www.pbs.org/newshour/nation/activists-reflect-on -1963-march-on-washington-amid-renewed-calls-to-address-racial -injustice.

2. Martin Luther King Jr., *The Autobiography of Martin Luther King, Jr.*, ed. Clayborne Carson (New York: Grand Central Publishing, 2001), 73.

3. King Jr., *Autobiography*, 137.

4. King Jr., *Autobiography*, 137.

5. C. S. Lewis, *The Screwtape Letters* (New York: HarperCollins, 2001), 171.

6. Kevin DeYoung, *Crazy Busy: A (Mercifully) Short Book About a (Really) Big Problem* (Wheaton, IL: Crossway, 2013), 82.

7. Ryan Holiday, *Stillness Is the Key* (New York: Portfolio, 2019), 33.

8. James F. Hoge Jr., "Media Pervasiveness," *Foreign Affairs*, July/August 1994, www.foreignaffairs.com/articles/united-states/1994-07-01/media -pervasiveness.

9. Steven Livingston, "Clarifying the CNN Effect: An Examination of Media Effects According to Type of Military Intervention," Joan Shorenstein Center on the Press, Politics, and Public Policy, John F. Kennedy School of Government, Harvard University, June 1997, 2, https:// shorensteincenter.org/wp-content/uploads/2012/03/r18_livingston.pdf.

10. Herbert A. Simon, "Designing Organizations for an Information-Rich World," in *Computers, Communications, and the Public Interest*,

ed. Martin Greenberger (Baltimore: Johns Hopkins Press, 1971), 40, https://digitalcollections.library.cmu.edu/awweb/awarchive ?type=file&item=33748.

11. Stephen R. Covey, *The 7 Habits of Highly Effective People*, 30th anniversary ed. (New York: Simon & Schuster, 2020), 119.

12. Fred Rogers, quoted in Holiday, *Stillness Is the Key*, 47.

13. Aaron Sorkin, interview by Bill Simmons, *The Bill Simmons Podcast*, episode 470, Ringer, January 18, 2019, https://www.theringer .com/the-bill-simmons-podcast/2019/1/18/18188058/aaron-sorkin-a -potential-rams-pats-sequel-kyries-leadership-and-million-dollar -nfl-picks-with-house.

14. Douglas H. Gresham, *Jack's Life: The Life Story of C. S. Lewis* (Nashville: Broadman, Holman, 2005), 8.

15. Cal Newport, *Deep Work: Rules for Focused Success in a Distracted World* (New York: Grand Central Publishing, 2016), 157.

16. Shawn Sprague, "Below Trend: The U.S. Productivity Slowdown Since the Great Recession," *Beyond the Numbers* 6, no. 2 (January 2017), www.bls.gov/opub/btn/volume-6/below-trend-the-us-productivity -slowdown-since-the-great-recession.htm.

17. Jean M. Twenge, "Have Smartphones Destroyed a Generation?," *Atlantic*, September 2017, www.theatlantic.com/magazine/archive/2017/09/ has-the-smartphone-destroyed-a-generation/534198.

18. Twenge, "Smartphones."

19. Twenge, "Smartphones."

20. Markham Heid, "You Asked: Is It Bad for You to Read the News Constantly?," *Time* magazine, May 19, 2020, https://time.com/5125894/ is-reading-news-bad-for-you.

21. Ron Dicker, "Hulk Hogan: 'Maybe We Don't Need a Vaccine' in Coronavirus Fight," *HuffPost*, April 7, 2020, www.huffpost.com/entry/hulk -hogan-vaccine-coronavirus_n_5e8c9874c5b62459a92f9530.

22. Jennifer Henderson, "750,000 People in North Carolina Could Be Infected by June, Warns State Health Official," *CNN*, April 6, 2020, www.cnn.com/world/live-news/coronavirus-pandemic-04-07-20/ h_400666f1056e4ba9a175ffb1add29b50.

23. John Mark Comer, *The Ruthless Elimination of Hurry* (Colorado Springs, CO: WaterBrook, 2019), 122.

24. Timothy Keller, *Encounters with Jesus: Unexpected Answers to Life's Biggest Questions* (New York: Penguin Books, 2013), 154.

25. Lewis, *Screwtape Letters*, 119–20.

26. Emily P. Freeman, *The Next Right Thing: A Simple, Soulful Practice for Making Life Decisions* (Grand Rapids, MI: Revell, 2019), chap. 2, Kindle.

27. Timothy Keller, interview with author, *The Call to Mastery*, April 14, 2020, https://podcast.jordanraynor.com/episodes/tim-keller-founder-of-redeemer-presbyterian-church/transcript.

28. Comer, *Ruthless Elimination*, 118.

29. Comer, *Ruthless Elimination*, 135.

30. Comer, *Ruthless Elimination*, 125.

31. Cal Newport, *Digital Minimalism: Choosing a Focused Life in a Noisy World* (New York: Portfolio, 2019), 9.

32. Richard John Neuhaus, *Freedom for Ministry* (Grand Rapids, MI: Eerdmans, 1979), 227.

33. DeYoung, *Crazy Busy*, 82–83.

34. Pablo Picasso, "What Life Has Taught Me," *Music Journal* 20, no. 1 (1962): 35.

35. Holiday, *Stillness Is the Key*, 32.

36. Jen Wilkin, *None Like Him: 10 Ways God Is Different from Us (and Why That's a Good Thing)* (Wheaton, IL: Crossway, 2016), 111–12.

37. Tim Ferriss, *The 4-Hour Workweek: Escape 9–5, Live Anywhere, and Join the New Rich* (New York: Harmony, 2009), 86.

38. Ralph Waldo Emerson, "Demonology," in *The Complete Works of Ralph Waldo Emerson: Lectures and Biographical Sketches* (Boston and New York: Houghton, Mifflin, 1904), 10:21.

39. Ferriss, *4-Hour Workweek*, 86.

40. Jack Knapp and John Zeratsky, *Make Time: How to Focus on What Matters Every Day* (New York: Currency, 2018), 4.

41. Professor W. Joseph Campbell, "Story of the Most Famous Seven Words in US Journalism," *BBC News*, February 10, 2012, www.bbc.com/news/world-us-canada-16918787.

42. Abraham Joshua Heschel, *The Sabbath*, FSG Classics (New York: Farrar, Straus & Giroux, 2005), 28.

43. Adrian F. Ward et al., "Brain Drain: The Mere Presence of One's Own Smartphone Reduces Available Cognitive Capacity," *Journal of the*

Association for Consumer Research 2, no. 2 (2017), www.journals.uchicago .edu/doi/abs/10.1086/691462.

44. Andy Crouch, *The Tech-Wise Family: Everyday Steps for Putting Technology in Its Proper Place* (Grand Rapids, MI: Baker, 2017), 34.

45. Comer, *Ruthless Elimination,* 227.

46. Mark Buchanan, *God Walk: Moving at the Speed of Your Soul* (Grand Rapids, MI: Zondervan, 2020), 6.

47. Buchanan, *God Walk,* 18.

48. King Jr., *Autobiography,* 29.

49. Søren Kierkegaard, *Letters and Documents,* trans. Henrik Rosenmeier (Princeton, NJ: Princeton University Press, 1978), 214.

50. Eric Metaxas, *Amazing Grace: William Wilberforce and the Heroic Campaign to End Slavery* (San Francisco: HarperCollins, 2007), 199.

51. Gresham, *Jack's Life,* 82.

52. Holiday, *Stillness Is the Key,* 197.

53. Buchanan, *God Walk,* 126.

54. You can listen to the full episode at JordanRaynor.com/RYT.

55. Brad Stone, *The Everything Store: Jeff Bezos and the Age of Amazon* (Boston: Little, Brown, 2013), prologue, Kindle.

56. Raymond M. Kethledge and Michael S. Erwin, *Lead Yourself First: Inspiring Leadership Through Solitude* (New York: Bloomsbury, 2017), chap. 2, Kindle.

57. Julia Cameron, "Morning Pages," *Artist's Way* (blog), April 19, 2017, https://juliacameronlive.com/2017/04/19/morning-pages-10.

Chapter 4: Prioritize Your Yeses

1. Tamika Catchings with Ken Petersen, *Catch a Star: Shining Through Adversity to Become a Champion* (Grand Rapids, MI: Revell, 2016), 41.

2. Catchings with Petersen, *Catch a Star,* 41.

3. Catchings with Petersen, *Catch a Star,* 41.

4. Catchings with Petersen, *Catch a Star,* 57.

5. Catchings with Petersen, *Catch a Star,* 165.

6. "Tamika Catchings," WNBA, www.wnba.com/player/tamika -catchings.

7. Catchings with Petersen, *Catch a Star,* 248.

8. Catchings with Petersen, *Catch a Star*, 202.

9. Dorothy L. Sayers, *The Man Born to Be King* (San Francisco: Ignatius Press, 1990), 89.

10. Kevin DeYoung, *Crazy Busy: A (Mercifully) Short Book About a (Really) Big Problem* (Wheaton, IL: Crossway, 2013), 55, 60.

11. Richard Koch, *The 80/20 Principle: The Secret to Achieving More with Less*, 3rd ed. (New York: Currency, 2011), 4.

12. John Maxwell, *Developing the Leader Within You* (Nashville: Thomas Nelson, 2012), 28.

13. Matt Perman, *What's Best Next: How the Gospel Transforms the Way You Get Things Done* (Grand Rapids, MI: Zondervan, 2014), 150.

14. Rick Warren, *The Purpose Driven Life: What on Earth Am I Here For?* (Grand Rapids, MI: Zondervan, 2002), 17–18.

15. *Mission: Impossible—Rogue Nation*, directed by Christopher McQuarrie (Hollywood, CA: Paramount Pictures, 2015).

16. Timothy Keller with Kathy Keller, *God's Wisdom for Navigating Life: A Year of Daily Devotions in the Book of Proverbs* (New York: Viking, 2017), 223.

17. John Doerr, *Measure What Matters: How Google, Bono, and the Gates Foundation Rock the World with OKRs* (New York: Portfolio, 2018), 10.

18. Jim Collins and Jerry I. Porras, *Built to Last: Successful Habits of Visionary Companies* (New York: HarperCollins, 2011), 9.

19. Doerr, *Measure What Matters*, 3.

20. "Gates' Law: How Progress Compounds and Why It Matters," *Farnam Street* (blog), May 2019, https://fs.blog/2019/05/gates-law.

21. Peter F. Drucker, *The Effective Executive: The Definitive Guide to Getting the Right Things Done* (New York: HarperCollins, 2006), 112.

22. David Brooks, "The Art of Focus," *New York Times*, June 2, 2014, www.nytimes.com/2014/06/03/opinion/brooks-the-art-of-focus.html.

23. New Story (website), https://newstorycharity.org.

24. Brett Hagler, interview with author, *The Call to Mastery*, April 21, 2020, https://podcast.jordanraynor.com/episodes/brett-hagler-co-founder-of-new-story-zA9N8iUX/transcript.

25. Steven Levy, "The Second Coming of Google's Larry Page," *Wired*, March 29, 2011, www.wired.co.uk/article/the-second-coming-of-larry-page.

26. Eric Schmidt, quoted in Doerr, *Measure What Matters*, 15.

27. Doerr, *Measure What Matters*, 7.

28. Doerr, *Measure What Matters*, 7.

29. Marissa Mayer, quoted in Steven Levy, *In the Plex: How Google Thinks, Works, and Shapes Our Lives* (New York: Simon & Schuster, 2011), 163.

30. Doerr, *Measure What Matters*, 50.

31. David Allen, *Getting Things Done: The Art of Stress-Free Productivity* (New York: Penguin Books, 2015), 273.

32. Warren Buffett, quoted in Jory MacKay, "This Brilliant Strategy Used by Warren Buffett Will Help You Prioritize Your Time," *Inc.*, November 15, 2017, www.inc.com/jory-mackay/warren-buffetts-personal-pilot-reveals-billionaires-brilliant-method-for-prioritizing.html.

33. Drucker, *Effective Executive*, 111.

34. Randy Alcorn, "Planned Neglect: Saying No to Good Things So We Can Say Yes to the Best," Eternal Perspective Ministries, May 18, 2008, www.epm.org/blog/2008/May/18/planned-neglect-saying-no-to-good-things-so-we-can.

Chapter 5: Accept Your "Unipresence"

1. Alister McGrath, *C. S. Lewis—A Life: Eccentric Genius, Reluctant Prophet* (Carol Stream, IL: Tyndale, 2013), 166.

2. Douglas H. Gresham, *Jack's Life: The Life Story of C. S. Lewis* (Nashville: Broadman, Holman, 2005), 149.

3. J. R. R. Tolkien, "From a Letter to Christopher Tolkien, 1 March 1944," in *The Letters of J. R. R. Tolkien*, ed. Humphrey Carpenter (Boston: Houghton Mifflin Harcourt, 2014), 68.

4. McGrath, *C. S. Lewis—A Life*, 66.

5. McGrath, *C. S. Lewis—A Life*, 75.

6. McGrath, *C. S. Lewis—A Life*, 86.

7. McGrath, *C. S. Lewis—A Life*, 95.

8. Gresham, *Jack's Life*, 74.

9. Gresham, *Jack's Life*, 75.

10. Gresham, *Jack's Life*, 75.

11. William O'Flaherty, "Lewis and Mrs. Moore Were Secret Lovers,"

Essential C. S. Lewis, June 10, 2017, https://essentialcslewis.com/2017/06/10/cmcsl-3-lewis-and-mrs-moore-were-secret-lovers/.

12. Gresham, *Jack's Life,* 140, 142.

13. Cal Newport, *Deep Work: Rules for Focused Success in a Distracted World* (New York: Grand Central Publishing, 2016), 3.

14. Eric Barker, "Stay Focused: 5 Ways to Increase Your Attention Span," *Barking Up the Wrong Tree* (blog), September 18, 2013, https://www.bakadesuyo.com/2013/09/stay-focused/.

15. Peter F. Drucker, *The Effective Executive: The Definitive Guide to Getting the Right Things Done* (New York: HarperCollins, 2006), 101–3.

16. Michael Hyatt, *Free to Focus: A Total Productivity System to Achieve More by Doing Less* (Grand Rapids, MI: Baker, 2019), 206.

17. Taylor Swift, "For Taylor Swift, the Future of Music Is a Love Story," *Wall Street Journal,* July 7, 2014, www.wsj.com/articles/for-taylor-swift-the-future-of-music-is-a-love-story-1404763219.

18. "'Infomania' Worse Than Marijuana," *BBC News,* April 22, 2005, http://news.bbc.co.uk/2/hi/uk_news/4471607.stm.

19. Newport, *Deep Work,* 41.

20. Sophie Leroy, "Why Is It So Hard to Do My Work? The Challenge of Attention Residue When Switching Between Work Tasks," *Organizational Behavior and Human Decision Processes* 109, no. 2 (July 2009): 168–81.

21. Newport, *Deep Work,* 6.

22. Sean Parker, quoted in Mike Allen, "Sean Parker Unloads on Facebook: 'God Only Knows What It's Doing to Our Children's Brains,'" Axios, November 9, 2017, www.axios.com/sean-parker-unloads-on-facebook-god-only-knows-what-its-doing-to-our-childrens-brains-1513306792-f855e7b4-4e99-4d60-8d51-2775559c2671.html.

23. "It's a Gamble: Dopamine Levels Tied to Uncertainty of Rewards," *Vanderbilt News,* May 7, 2004, https://news.vanderbilt.edu/2004/05/07/its-a-gamble-dopamine-levels-tied-to-uncertainty-of-rewards-59664.

24. Bill Maher, "New Rule: Social Media Is the New Nicotine | Real Time with Bill Maher (HBO)," video, 4:54, May 12, 2017, www.youtube.com/watch?v=KDqoTDM7tio.

25. *The Social Network,* directed by David Fincher, screenplay by Aaron Sorkin (Culver City, CA: Columbia Pictures, 2010).

26. Jen Wilkin, *None Like Him: 10 Ways God Is Different from Us (and Why That's a Good Thing)* (Wheaton, IL: Crossway, 2016), 99.

27. Kevin DeYoung, *Crazy Busy: A (Mercifully) Short Book About a (Really) Big Problem* (Wheaton, IL: Crossway, 2013), 88.

28. Tony Schwartz with Jean Tomes and Catherine McCarthy, *The Way We're Working Isn't Working: The Four Forgotten Needs That Energize Great Performance* (New York: Free Press, 2010), 190.

29. "Can We Chat? Instant Messaging Apps Invade the Workplace," ReportLinker, June 8, 2017, www.reportlinker.com/insight/instant-messaging-apps-invade-workplace.html.

30. Ryan Holiday, *Stillness Is the Key* (New York: Portfolio, 2019), 30.

31. John Mark Comer, *The Ruthless Elimination of Hurry* (Colorado Springs, CO: WaterBrook, 2019), 227.

32. David Allen, *Getting Things Done: The Art of Stress-Free Productivity* (New York: Penguin Books, 2015), 108.

33. Drucker, *Effective Executive*, 29.

34. Malcolm Gladwell, *Outliers: The Story of Success* (Boston: Little, Brown, 2008), 39.

35. Schwartz with Tomes and McCarthy, *Way We're Working*, 6.

36. Roy F. Baumeister and John Tierney, *Willpower: Rediscovering the Greatest Human Strength* (New York: Penguin Books, 2012), 23.

37. Matthew Walker, *Why We Sleep: Unlocking the Power of Sleep and Dreams* (New York: Scribner, 2017), 143.

38. Newport, *Deep Work*, 150.

39. C. S. Lewis, "[Letter to Arthur Greeves,] 20 December 1943," in *Yours, Jack: Spiritual Direction from C. S. Lewis,* ed. Paul F. Ford (San Francisco: HarperCollins, 2008), 97–98.

Chapter 6: Embrace Productive Rest

1. Shay Cochrane (CEO of Social Squares), in discussion with the author, September 2020.

2. Cochrane, discussion with author.

3. Cochrane, discussion with author.

4. Cochrane, discussion with author.

5. Cochrane, discussion with author.

6. Tony Schwartz with Jean Tomes and Catherine McCarthy, *The Way We're Working Isn't Working: The Four Forgotten Needs That Energize Great Performance* (New York: Free Press, 2010), x.

7. Leonardo da Vinci, quoted in Heidi Foster, "Heidi Foster: Do Better at Work by Leaving It," *Reno Gazette Journal,* July 19, 2014, www.rgj.com/story/money/business/2014/07/19/heidi-foster-better-work-leaving/12898465.

8. Schwartz with Tomes and McCarthy, *Way We're Working,* 111.

9. Schwartz with Tomes and McCarthy, *Way We're Working,* 6.

10. "2013 International Bedroom Poll: Summary of Findings," National Sleep Foundation, 7, www.sleepfoundation.org/wp-content/uploads/2018/10/RPT495a.pdf.

11. Saverio Stranges et al., "Sleep Problems: An Emerging Global Epidemic? Findings from the INDEPTH WHO-SAGE Study Among More Than 40,000 Older Adults from 8 Countries Across Africa and Asia," *Sleep* 35, no. 8 (August 1, 2012): 1173–81, www.ncbi.nlm.nih.gov/pmc/articles/PMC3397790.

12. Walker, *Why We Sleep,* 7, 138.

13. Walker, *Why We Sleep,* 3.

14. National Institute of Neurological Disorders and Stroke, "Brain Basics: Understanding Sleep," National Institutes of Health, August 13, 2019, www.ninds.nih.gov/Disorders/Patient-Caregiver-Education/Understanding-sleep.

15. Scott A. Cairney, quoted in Ana Sandoiu, "Can You Learn in Your Sleep? Yes, and Here's How," Medical News Today, March 8, 2018, www.medicalnewstoday.com/articles/321161.

16. Walker, *Why We Sleep,* 126.

17. Matthew Gibson and Jeffrey Shrader, "Time Use and Productivity: The Wage Returns to Sleep," *Wall Street Journal,* July 10, 2014, https://online.wsj.com/public/resources/documents/091814sleep.pdf.

18. Rachel Gillett, "Larry Page Created Google in His Sleep—Here's Why 'Sleeping On It' Can Be Legitimately Productive," Yahoo! Finance, May 5, 2016, https://finance.yahoo.com/news/productive-while-youre-sleeping-125100995.html?guccounter=1.

19. Walker, *Why We Sleep,* 221.

20. Stacy Conradt, "Creative Breakthroughs That Came During Sleep,"

Atlantic, October 12, 2012, www.theatlantic.com/health/archive/2012/10/creative-breakthroughs-that-came-during-sleep/263562.

21. Jeffrey Kluger, "The Spark of Invention," *Time* magazine, November 14, 2013, https://techland.time.com/2013/11/14/the-spark-of-invention.

22. Walker, *Why We Sleep,* 228.

23. Walker, *Why We Sleep,* 228.

24. Walker, *Why We Sleep,* 228.

25. Walker, *Why We Sleep,* 132.

26. Walker, *Why We Sleep,* 227.

27. Walker, *Why We Sleep,* 229.

28. D. A. Carson, *Scandalous: The Cross and the Resurrection of Jesus* (Wheaton, IL: Crossway, 2010), 147.

29. Joseph Ware, "Emigrants' Guide to California, 1849," Donner Summit Historical Society, http://www.donnersummithistoricalsociety.org/pages/bookreviews/EmigrantsGuide.html.

30. Dee Ann Turner, *Bet on Talent: How to Create a Remarkable Culture That Wins the Hearts of Customers* (Grand Rapids, MI: Baker, 2019), 53.

31. Dan Buettner, quoted in Ryan Buxton, "What Seventh-Day Adventists Get Right That Lengthens Their Life Expectancy," *HuffPost,* July 31, 2014, www.huffpost.com/entry/seventh-day-adventists-life-expectancy_n_5638098.

32. Dr. Wayne Dysinger, quoted in Peter Bowes, "Loma Linda: The Secret to a Long Healthy life?," *BBC News,* December 8, 2014, www.bbc.com/news/magazine-30351406.

33. John Mark Comer, *The Ruthless Elimination of Hurry* (Colorado Springs, CO: WaterBrook, 2019), 157.

34. Ryder Carroll, *The Bullet Journal Method: Track the Past, Order the Present, Design the Future* (New York: Portfolio, 2018), 43.

35. Abraham Joshua Heschel, *The Sabbath,* FSG Classics (New York: Farrar, Straus & Giroux, 2005), 29.

36. "The Sabbath: God's Gift of Rest," Seventh-Day Adventist Church, www.adventist.org/the-sabbath/the-gift-of-sabbath-rest-the-sabbath-was-made-for-us.

37. DeYoung, *Crazy Busy,* 91.

38. N. T. Wright, *Surprised by Hope: Rethinking Heaven, the Resurrection, and the Mission of the Church* (New York: HarperCollins, 2018), 262.

39. Martin Gilbert, *Churchill: A Life* (New York: Henry Holt, 1991), 486.

40. Winston S. Churchill, *Thoughts and Adventures: Churchill Reflects on Spies, Cartoons, Flying, and the Future,* ed. James W. Muller (Wilmington, DE: Intercollegiate Studies Institute, 2009), 323.

41. Joel Manby, interview with author, *The Call to Mastery,* May 5, 2020, https://podcast.jordanraynor.com/episodes/joel-manby-fmr-ceo-of -seaworld/transcript.

42. Manby, interview with author.

43. Michael Hyatt, *Free to Focus: A Total Productivity System to Achieve More by Doing Less* (Grand Rapids, MI: Baker, 2019), 71.

44. I got this from Will Weatherford, the former Speaker of the House of Representatives for the state of Florida. See Will Weatherford, interview with author, *The Call to Mastery,* May 12, 2020, https://podcast .jordanraynor.com/episodes/will-weatherford-fmr-speaker-of-the -florida-house-_TXOu_3H/transcript.

45. Walker, *Why We Sleep,* 137.

46. Walker, *Why We Sleep,* 140.

47. Diane S. Lauderdale et al., "Objectively Measured Sleep Characteristics Among Early-Middle-Aged Adults: The CARDIA Study," *American Journal of Epidemiology* 164, no. 1 (July 1, 2006): 5–16, https://academic .oup.com/aje/article/164/1/5/81104.

48. Siobhan Banks and David F. Dinges, "Behavioral and Physiological Consequences of Sleep Restriction," *Journal of Clinical Sleep Medicine* 3, no. 5 (August 15, 2007): 519–28, www.ncbi.nlm.nih.gov/pmc/articles/ PMC1978335.

49. Jason Alvarez, "'Short Sleep' Gene Prevents Memory Deficits Associated with Sleep Deprivation," University of California San Francisco Health, October 16, 2019, www.ucsf.edu/news/2019/10/415671/short -sleep-gene-prevents-memory-deficits-associated-sleep-deprivation.

50. Neil Herndon, "The Odds Are Against You: Things More Likely Than Winning the Powerball," *Forbes,* January 13, 2016, www.forbes.com/ sites/archenemy/2016/01/13/the-odds-are-against-you-things-more -likely-than-winning-the-powerball/?sh=2ea43ec44468.

51. "Sleep Better Now: 43 Tips We Need More Than Ever," *Wall Street Journal,* March 22, 2020, https://graphics.wsj.com/image-grid/off -duty-50-spring-2020.

52. "Take Advantage of Toasty Toes," *Wall Street Journal,* March 22, 2020, https://graphics.wsj.com/image-grid/off-duty-50-spring-2020/8534/take-advantage-of-toasty-toes.

53. "Hang Calming Botanical Wallpaper in Your Bedroom," *Wall Street Journal,* March 22, 2020, https://graphics.wsj.com/image-grid/off-duty-50-spring-2020/8548/hang-calming-botanical-wallpaper-in-your-bedroom.

54. "Fantasize About a Ludicrously Extravagant Mink Sleep Mask," *Wall Street Journal,* March 22, 2020, https://graphics.wsj.com/image-grid/off-duty-50-spring-2020/8536/fantasize-about-a-ludicrously-extravagant-mink-sleep-mask.

55. Maurice M. Ohayon et al., "Meta-Analysis of Quantitative Sleep Parameters from Childhood to Old Age in Healthy Individuals: Developing Normative Sleep Values Across the Human Lifespan," *Sleep* 27, no. 7 (October 2004): 1255–73, https://academic.oup.com/sleep/article/27/7/1255/2696819.

56. Walker, *Why We Sleep,* 96.

57. Sophie Desjardins et al., "Factors Involved in Sleep Efficiency: A Population-Based Study of Community-Dwelling Elderly Persons," *Sleep* 42, no. 5 (May 2019), www.ncbi.nlm.nih.gov/pmc/articles/PMC6519908.

58. Walker, *Why We Sleep,* 35.

59. Danielle Pacheco, "Alcohol and Sleep," Sleep Foundation, September 4, 2020, www.sleepfoundation.org/nutrition/alcohol-and-sleep.

60. Sally Lloyd-Jones, *The Jesus Storybook Bible: Every Story Whispers His Name* (Grand Rapids, MI: Zondervan, 2007), 36.

Chapter 7: Eliminate All Hurry

1. Maxwell King, interview with author, *The Call to Mastery,* February 18, 2020, https://podcast.jordanraynor.com/episodes/maxwell-king-mister-rogers-biographer.

2. King, interview with author.

3. Maxwell King, *The Good Neighbor: The Life and Work of Fred Rogers* (New York: Abrams, 2019), 8.

4. King, *Good Neighbor,* 8.

5. Ryan Holiday, *Stillness Is the Key* (New York: Portfolio, 2019), 45.

6. Lisa Dormire, quoted in King, *Good Neighbor,* 120.

7. Arthur W. Pink, *Why Four Gospels?* (Edinburgh, Scotland: CrossReach Publications, 2018), 36.

8. "John 11:9," *Cambridge Bible for Schools and Colleges,* Bible Hub, https:// biblehub.com/commentaries/john/11-9.htm.

9. Kevin DeYoung, *Crazy Busy: A (Mercifully) Short Book About a (Really) Big Problem* (Wheaton, IL: Crossway, 2013), 54–55.

10. John Ortberg, *Soul Keeping: Caring for the Most Important Part of You* (Grand Rapids, MI: Zondervan, 2014), chap. 11, Kindle.

11. Dallas Willard, quoted in Ortberg, *Soul Keeping,* introduction, Kindle.

12. "How to Create a Zero-Based Budget," Ramsey Solutions, December 17, 2020, www.daveramsey.com/blog/how-to-make-a-zero-based -budget.

13. "How to Create a Zero-Based Budget."

14. Matt Perman, *What's Best Next: How the Gospel Transforms the Way You Get Things Done* (Grand Rapids, MI: Zondervan, 2014), 52.

15. Rachel Cruze, "15 Practical Budgeting Tips," Ramsey Solutions, December 11, 2020, www.daveramsey.com/blog/the-truth-about -budgeting.

16. Mason Currey, *Daily Rituals: How Artists Work* (New York: Knopf, 2013).

17. David Brooks, "The Good Order," *New York Times,* September 25, 2014, www.nytimes.com/2014/09/26/opinion/david-brooks-routine -creativity-and-president-obamas-un-speech.html.

18. King, interview with author.

19. King, interview with author.

20. King, interview with author.

21. Tom Junod, quoted in King, *Good Neighbor,* 312.

22. Greg McKeown, *Essentialism: The Disciplined Pursuit of Less* (New York: Currency, 2020), 207–8.

23. Vincent Carlos, "Why So Many Successful People Wear the Same Outfit Every Day," *Thrive Global,* May 30, 2019, https://thriveglobal .com/stories/why-successful-people-often-wear-the-same-outfit -every-day.

24. Bradley Blakeman (former scheduler for President George W. Bush), in discussion with the author, June 2020.

25. John Pencavel, quoted in Bob Sullivan, "Memo to Work Martyrs: Long Hours Make You Less Productive," CNBC, January 26, 2015, www.cnbc.com/2015/01/26/working-more-than-50-hours-makes-you-less-productive.html.

26. Matthew Walker, *Why We Sleep: Unlocking the Power of Sleep and Dreams* (New York: Scribner, 2017), 19.

27. Walker, *Why We Sleep*, 20.

28. Laura Scroggs, "The Eisenhower Matrix," Todoist, https://todoist.com/productivity-methods/eisenhower-matrix.

29. Saint Francis of Assisi, quoted in *Reader's Digest* 130, no. 777–782 (1987), 33.

30. Timothy Keller (@timkellernyc), "Self-control is the ability to do the important thing rather than the urgent thing," Twitter, June 14, 2018, 12:39 p.m., https://twitter.com/timkellernyc/status/1007331589800562688.

31. Adapted from McKeown, *Essentialism*, 190. All credit goes to him for the thinking behind these words.

32. Need proof? Read up on the "planning fallacy" at Daniel Kahneman and Amos Tversky, *Intuitive Prediction: Biases and Correction Procedures* (Arlington, VA: Advanced Decision Technology, 1977), 2-2, https://apps.dtic.mil/dtic/tr/fulltext/u2/a047747.pdf.

33. Derek Sivers, *Anything You Want: 40 Lessons for a New Kind of Entrepreneur* (New York: Portfolio, 2015), 13.

34. Mark Batterson, *Win the Day: 7 Daily Habits to Help You Stress Less and Accomplish More* (Colorado Springs, CO: Multnomah, 2020), 85–86.

35. Emily P. Freeman, *The Next Right Thing: A Simple, Soulful Practice for Making Life Decisions* (Grand Rapids, MI: Revell, 2019), chap. 16, Kindle.

36. Richard Branson (@richardbranson), "Opportunities are like buses—there's always another one coming," Twitter, November 1, 2012, 12:13 p.m., https://twitter.com/richardbranson/status/264067714266587136?lang=en.

37. Adapted from Kevin DeYoung, *Crazy Busy*, 40–41.

38. Jony Ive, quoted in Vlad Savov, "Watch This: Apple's Imperfect

Video About Perfection," Verge, June 11, 2013, www.theverge.com/2013/6/11/4418242/apple-imperfect-video-about-perfection.

39. Jimmy Collins, quoted in Dee Ann Turner, *Bet on Talent: How to Create a Remarkable Culture That Wins the Hearts of Customers* (Grand Rapids, MI: Baker, 2019), 113.

40. Turner, *Bet on Talent*, 186.

Epilogue: The Dark Side of Discipline

1. Timothy Keller, *The Prodigal God: Recovering the Heart of the Christian Faith* (New York: Penguin Books, 2008), 61.

2. Keller, *Prodigal God*, 61.

ABOUT THE AUTHOR

JORDAN RAYNOR is a serial entrepreneur and national best-selling author who helps Christians do their most exceptional work for the glory of God and the good of others. Through his books, podcast, and weekly devotionals, Jordan has helped millions of Christians in every single country connect the gospel to their work.

In addition to producing this content, Jordan serves as the executive chairman of Threshold 360, a venture-backed tech start-up that has built the world's largest library of 360-degree experiences of hotels, restaurants, and attractions. Jordan previously served as CEO of the company, following a string of successful ventures of his own.

Jordan has been selected twice as a Google Fellow and served in the White House under President George W. Bush. A highly sought-after public speaker on the topic of faith and work, Jordan has spoken at Harvard University, SXSW, and many other high-profile events around the world.

A sixth-generation Floridian, Jordan lives in Tampa with his wife, Kara, and their three young daughters: Ellison, Kate, and Emery.

ABOUT THE TYPE

THIS BOOK was set in Caslon, a typeface first designed in 1722 by William Caslon (1692–1766). Its widespread use by most English printers in the early eighteenth century soon supplanted the Dutch typefaces that had formerly prevailed. The roman is considered a "workhorse" typeface due to its pleasant, open appearance, while the italic is exceedingly decorative.

Stop Doing It All
So You Can Do
What Matters Most

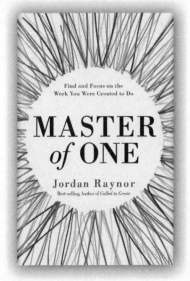

In a world of limitless options, discover how to find and excel at the one thing you were made to do exceptionally well in service to God and others.

The solution isn't to do more—it's to become a master of one.

WATERBROOK

Free Resources to Help Redeem Your Time

Join more than 100,000 others and receive my free weekly devotional, *The Word Before Work*, where we connect the gospel to our efforts to redeem our time. Sign-up at **JordanRaynor.com/TWBW.**

Principles never change, but practices do. Keep up with the latest and subscribe to my podcast, *The Call to Mastery*, at **JordanRaynor.com/podcast.**

@jordanraynor